THE NEW **VEGETARIAN**

A wide ranging, practical guide to vegetarianism and the issues it raises for all those who have just given up meat or who are thinking of doing so.

D1346893

THE NEW VEGETARIAN

The Complete Survival Plan for Those Who Have Given Up Meat

by

Michael Cox

With Recipes
by

Desda Crockett

Illustrated by Clive Birch

THORSONS PUBLISHERS LIMITED
Wellingborough, Northamptonshire

Produced in co-operation with
The Vegetarian Society of the United Kingdom Ltd.
Parkdale, Dunham Road, Altrincham, Cheshire

First published September 1985
Second Impression December 1985
Third Impression April 1986

British Library Cataloguing in Publication Data

Cox, Michael, *1948-*
   The new vegetarian.
   1. Vegetarianism
   I. Title   II. Crockett, Desda
   613.2'62   TX392

ISBN 0-7225-1106-X

Printed and bound in Great Britain

CONTENTS

For DJY.
Our first convert!

Vegetarians have wicked, shifty eyes, and laugh in a cold and calculating manner. They pinch little children, steal stamps, drink water, favour beards . . . wheeze, squeak, drawl and maunder.

J. B. Morton ('Beachcomber'), *By the Way*.

INTRODUCTION

IN 1890, at a meeting held under the auspices of the West Ham Vegetarian Society, vegetarians and carnivores put their respective ideologies to the test.

The occasion was reported with gusto by the *Cambridge Review* — no doubt with the predominantly carnivorous prejudices of its Varsity readers firmly in mind. 'The proceedings appear to have been of a rather mixed character,' said the Review facetiously. 'A hymn was sung, the drum and fife band "performed a selection for the delectation of the assembly", and the chairman preached the benefits of vegetarianism.'

After an affecting offering from the children's choir came the main event: a tug of war between vegetarians and carnivores. There were three rounds. In the first, three vegetarians vanquished four carnivores; in the second, six carnivores managed to pull over four vegetarians; but in the last and spectacularly conclusive round, six carnivores were pulled right over the line by a squad of victorious vegetable eaters. 'The champions of "roast beef",' said the *Cambridge Review,* 'retired discomfited, sadder and, let us hope, wiser men.'

The tug of war, metaphorically speaking, is still going on today. On the one side are ranged the committed vegetarians, increasingly supported by nutritional, medical, and economic facts. On the other are the — equally committed — carnivores, supported by their own powerful pressure groups, strong and sure in the realization that for the time being they are still numerically superior — though the balance is shifting significantly — and that they have a long and sturdy weight of tradition to back them up.

When this book first appeared in 1979 we put forward the idea of 'subverting' meat-eaters. In six years the situation has changed dramatically. Vegetarians no longer need to deploy the subtle subversive tactics we advocated then: the meat-eating habit is now under attack from many sides. The general public is far better informed than it has ever been in the past about basic nutritional facts; about the scandal of unnecessary food additives; about the link between certain diets and degenerative disease, allergic reactions, and hyperactivity in children; as well as about the overwhelming ethical and ecological arguments in favour of vegetarianism.

Today, the vegetarian 'minority' is a force to be reckoned with, and its influence is growing all the time. This is why we have changed the emphasis and tone of the book. Vegetarians no longer need to be defensive or apologetic about their convictions, and so the text has been revised and rewritten to provide the ever growing number of new vegetarians with a handy guide to the many issues involved in cutting meat out of one's diet, rather than, as in the previous edition, with suggestions for converting — or subverting — others.

These issues may well be irrelevant for some people: there are a host of reasons for giving up meat, all of them in the end valid. But for many more people, giving up meat is more than a simple emotional reaction — it is more than just 'feeling sorry for animals'. Because of the widespread awareness of the issues, people are working out where they stand on the vegetarian question in much greater detail. We hope this book will help both new vegetarians *and* those who are moving towards reducing their meat intake significantly to find intellectual, as well as moral and culinary, satisfaction in vegetarianism.

There is still resentment, misapprehension, ignorance, and downright hostility towards those who have opted for the vegetarian alternative; but the mood is changing. Vegetarians are, and need to be, better informed, and knowledge invariably deepens conviction. If you have just given up meat, we hope this book will help clarify your personal decision for doing so; if you are moving towards vegetarianism, but have not yet fully taken the plunge, we hope you will find food for thought, and the incentive to push on towards living without meat altogether. Most new vegetarians suffer from crises of confidence at some point or other, and it is only gradually that you begin to realize that the step you have taken is not a leap into the dark. You may be worried about the sufficiency of your new diet.

Are you getting enough protein? What about Vitamin B_{12}? Is it necessary to follow through the logic of vegetarianism and become a vegan, or a fruitarian? What would happen if everyone opted for vegetarianism? How does my vegetarianism affect other people? Am I ethically justified in giving up meat? Have I landed myself with a morally improving but boring diet?

These are the sort of questions that can bother the new vegetarian, either on his or her own account, or because other people insist on raising them. This book offers some answers, as well as a selection of simple, workaday recipes designed to fit in with a busy modern lifestyle. The Reading List provides a selection of cookbooks for those who wish to experiment with the immense range and variety of vegetarian cuisine. The recipes offered here can be prepared quickly and easily and require no exotic ingredients or special skill. One common fallacy is that vegetarian food is fiddly and complicated to prepare, whereas almost anyone can put together a meal whose main ingredient is meat. The truth is that giving up meat is neither a deprivation nor an imposition, and preparing quick, nourishing, and *interesting* meals is a great deal easier without meat than with it. One further feature of the recipes, for those who have not yet totally committed themselves, is that they blend easily and unobtrusively with a meat diet.

Vegetarianism, it has been said, is a form of boycott. To make the boycott of cruel and fundamentally unnecessary farming methods successful a vegetarian must never be shy about his or her refusal to eat meat. A vegetarian in an omnivorous society is always being asked about the reasons for his strange diet. This can be irritating, or even embarrassing; but it also provides an opportunity for enlightenment: an opportunity for telling people who may not have thought about it exactly why the vegetarian alternative is the *only* alternative to the immoral and wholly unnecessary slaughter of our fellow creatures.

1.

BREAKING THE MOULD

THERE is nothing more calculated to stiffen a carnivore's resistance to a reform of his diet than a ranting, holier-than-thou vegetarian who sees life as a constant vigil against eating or drinking anything that he knows, or suspects, is either detrimental to his physical system, or inimical to his tender moral conscience. A common complaint by meat-eaters that vegetarians are dour killjoys sometimes has a basis in fact, and the taunt 'If you don't smoke, drink, or eat meat, what do you do?' may occasionally be justified. The dedicated carnivore, from one point of view, has at least the positive virtue of enjoying his food; and though the reasons for giving up the consumption of animal flesh are becoming increasingly irresistible, an unashamed satisfaction in putting away a pound of rump steak is, perhaps, preferable to the faddist who worries himself silly over every mouthful.

But whence comes the conviction that meat — any sort of meat, no matter how far removed from the flesh of real animals — is good for us? What is the source of the meat-eater's confidence that vegetarians are 'abnormal' and of the power that meat has over the popular imagination?

Lord Byron, in *Don Juan*, made the connection between the English fondness for meat and their warlike disposition — between, as he put it, 'beef' and 'battle'. Carnivores today, reacting purely on inherited and instinctive prejudice, still make a similar, if unconscious, connection. For them, a person who does not eat meat is taking a dangerous line: they believe that the vegetarian is denying his body something vital, something inescapably essential. This is a fallacy, but the feeling is part of a primitive reflex, a residual, implicit belief in the power of blood.

To some extent we all share this belief, since it is ingrained in us — an instinct peculiar to the species. From the dawn of human consciousness men associated blood with life and the cessation of its function with the extinction of life. As it flowed from the body, so life itself ebbed away. The identification of blood with the life force deepened until blood became a symbol of the soul, a stream that carried with it the spiritual as well as the physical nature of Man.

From this association of blood and being arose the taboos on specific foods — such as the prohibition against eating the flesh of certain animals by the Jews. These taboos were based on the belief that to take in the blood of an animal was, in some sense, to absorb its nature.

Other societies, however, took a different view based on the same reasoning. They saw blood as a source of power. To drink the blood of a powerful enemy (or, as the Masai warriors did, to drink the blood of lions) was to assimilate his strength; similarly, to eat your enemy's brains, as the headhunters of Borneo did, was to take advantage of his mental powers and make them one's own.

All this has had a peculiar and little considered consequence for vegetarians living in the latter half of the twentieth century. With these beliefs imprinted on the collective unconscious, it is easy to understand the fears that meat-eaters feel at the prospect of giving up what a primitive logic tells them to be a source of essential strength. Behind those fears is a vast web of associations, superstitions, and cultural attitudes.

The concept of blood as the river of life continues to exert a powerful psychological hold even today. It is a force that no vegetarian should underestimate. It perhaps underlies the general disinclination of the average housewife to provide her family with soya protein instead of chunks of stewing steak: no amount of arguing about the nutritional sufficiency of soya products, it seems, can overcome what must be seen as an unconscious belief in the benefits of bloody flesh.

Vegetarians, therefore, are people who have managed to conquer this mythopoeic belief in the regenerative power of blood and flesh. This 'abnormality' goes some way towards accounting for the sense of apartness, even of alienation, that vegetarians sometimes feel. It is, after all, an extreme step to place oneself voluntarily outside the circle of ingrained beliefs and assumptions within which most of the tribe live in contented prejudice. Little wonder that people look upon you with amazement or incredulity, or sheer hostility: in essence, the vegetarian has become a renegade — figuratively, and sometimes literally, an outsider.

The power of these primitive, deeply ingrained prejudices has not been fully taken into account in the great debate on the pros and cons of vegetarianism. It is, nonetheless, a substantial barrier to those who long for a completely vegetarian world. Think for a moment of that imposing and resonant figure, Count Dracula:

> The vampire bites his victims; and anyone with the slightest knowledge of Freud knows that a bite is a sado-erotic kiss; in *Dracula* the female vampires around Jonathan Harker's bed comment that his health and strength mean 'kisses for us all' . . . Blood is profoundly involved with sexuality in man's psyche . . . And modern psychology has shown the predominance of blood and blood-letting in the erotic fantasies of many psychiatric patients. [1]

Regenerative power, the acquisition of strength and intelligence, and now the unleashing of erotic fantasies . . . With all these potent images and associations ranged against him it is little wonder the vegetarian occasionally begins to wilt under the enormous psychological pressures that society's collective unconscious is capable of applying.

The mention of Dracula is not a trivializing irrelevance. Blood is the very stuff of physical life, and meat partakes of its qualities and of its mythical and psychological resonances. Sometimes no amount of logical argument, or the presentation of factual evidence, can overcome this primordial conviction.

Parents and Children

Espousing the vegetarian cause as a thinking mature adult is one thing; taking the decision to give up meat on behalf of an unborn child is, for many people, quite another.

If you are a newly converted vegetarian mother-to-be you will have quite legitimate worries about the sufficiency of your new diet for your baby. The straight answer to the question, 'Is a vegetarian diet safe for pregnant women *and* their babies?' is, 'Yes' — that is, if you take certain obvious precautions.

In fact there are specific advantages in a vegetarian diet during pregnancy. For one thing, you will tend to get the required amount of folic acid, a vitamin that is 50 to 90 per cent destroyed by cooking, since vegetarians eat more of the raw fruits and vegetables that supply folic acid. Fibre, too, is generally more plentiful in a vegetarian diet, and this is especially important during pregnancy when food moves more slowly through the digestive tract.

On the whole, vegetarians are more 'health conscious' than non-vegetarians, and thus are less likely to load themselves with empty calorie- and additive-laden foods during pregnancy — a time when every mouthful should count nutritionally.

However — and this cannot be stressed too much — care is needed. If you are a pregnant vegetarian you should make sure that you obtain the following basic nutrients in the correct amounts: protein, calcium, iron, vitamin B_{12}, vitamin B, vitamin C, vitamin B_6 (riboflavin), vitamin D, and vitamin E. Make sure your diet is well balanced *before* pregnancy; take sensible exercise, and take vitamin and mineral supplements if so advised. Above all, if you are at all worried that your diet is insufficient in some way seek expert medical and nutritional advice as early as possible.

These are the essential practical measures every vegetarian mother should take, and the nutritional aspects of vegetarianism will be covered in more detail in Chapter 3. Whether or not she has a right to impose her beliefs on a developing foetus or a growing child who has no say in the matter is another question. The best answer to this is to point out that it is no different morally to imposing a meat diet on an infant who may very well decide in adulthood to become a vegetarian.

There are, of course, dangers in adhering to too strict an ideology. These were given wide prominence in 1979 by a report in the *British Medical Journal* provocatively titled 'Malnutrition in Infants Receiving Cult Diets: A Form of Child Abuse'. The report's summary was as follows:

> Severe nutritional disorders, including kwashiorkor, marasmus, and rickets, were seen in four children and were due to parental food faddism, which should perhaps be regarded as a form of child abuse. All disorders were corrected with more normal diets and vitamin supplements.
>
> In view of the potentially serious consequences of restricted diets being fed to children, families at risk should be identified and

acceptable nutritional advice given. When children are found to be suffering from undernutrition due to personal food faddism a court order will normally be a necessary step in providing adequate treatment and supervision.

This is damning enough on the face of it. However, the parents involved in the four case reports were certainly extreme in their dietary views. In the first case, for instance, the parents were converts to a cult whose main dietary prescription was an adherence to a restricted, uncooked vegetable diet, and the child had received only breast milk and uncooked fruit and vegetables. More importantly, it is not just those on 'cult' or 'faddist' diets that suffer from malnutrition: large numbers of children on so-called normal diets suffer in the same way by consuming large quantities of foods that are deficient in essential nutrients.

The inevitable publicity given to this kind of report is of course worrying to new vegetarians, though perhaps less so now than in 1979. But no vegetarian mother should be anxious that the diet she has adopted will have an adverse effect on her children. There are several excellent books offering guidance on pre-conceptual, pre-natal, and post-natal nutrition (see the Reading List); if you are still worried, the Vegetarian Society can advise you. Just remember that, with only a modicum of common sense, babies brought up on a vegetarian diet are every bit as healthy, if not healthier, than those who grow up with the taste of blood in their mouths.

Diet and Disease

Malnutrition, then, is not confined to the underdeveloped Third World. It is one of the greatest ironies of our time that in America, the apotheosis of the developed country, where hardly anyone actually starves, the danger of undernourishment — of malnutrition in a strict sense — is high. Though we in the West consume vast quantities of edible substances, what many of those substances actually provide in nutritional terms is, at best, adequate; at worst, positively dangerous.

For many modern families, too much is consumed of what gives too little in nutritional benefit. Taste — that is, what pleases us — and convenience take precedence over what is good for us; indeed being told that something is good for us often stiffens the resolve to have nothing to do with it — like a child who is told to eat breadcrusts in order to have curly hair.

But there is a breaking point, which we now seem to be approaching fast. Medical evidence of the link between diet and diseases such as cancer and heart failure is accumulating and is becoming known to more and more people. Inadequate dietary patterns combined with life styles that do little or nothing to keep the body in optimum health have led to a deadly harvest of disease and debility. Becoming a vegetarian is a key factor in any attempt to break away from dietary patterns whose inadequacy is now clear.

Ignorance about what we eat is a fact of life. It goes hand in hand with a general ignorance of what goes on inside our bodies. Of course we do not actually need to think about the way our bodies miraculously continue to function day after day. We only become aware of our internal mechanisms when they impinge on our consciousness — usually when something goes wrong.

But we cannot, and should not, remain aloof from our bodies. Every single day we are all responsible for refuelling the physical system, and doing what is best for our bodies would seem the only logical and sensible course; but in fact many people in the developed world give little thought to the vital question of what is best for them. They simply remain content to eat what pleases them.

Historically, humans learned by trial and error which things were good to eat and which were to be avoided. We are the inheritors of centuries of accumulated wisdom. We know, for instance, that bread is good for us, being made from a grain that, since the earliest civilizations, has been established as a staple and nutritious food. But once we remove ourselves from a direct experience of the primary source, then our instinctive trust in the nutritional value of bread is misplaced and prompts us to consume some very strange creations indeed.

We are now moving away from thinking of bread only in terms of thin, white slices of cellophane-wrapped pap, and consumer pressure means that it is now possible to buy bread in a high street supermarket that has not had all its essential fibre and natural nutrients refined out of it. But bread is only one example of how in recent years the food industry has driven a wedge between the consumer and natural products. The convenience foods that are still eaten in such vast quantities are at several removes from nature. Just look around you at what people are putting into their baskets next time you are in a supermarket: in spite of all the media attention given to health matters — such as the success of a book like *E for Additives,* which documents the iniquitous use of generally unnecessary additives in the majority of staple convenience products — the preponderance of devitalized and denatured foods is still glaringly obvious. People still apparently believe that because something is edible it is, by some occult process, sufficient for the body's needs. White bread is edible, but it is not nutritious: charcoal-broiled steaks are edible, but eating them regularly may be as dangerous as smoking.

The issues we have just touched upon are part of the overall context of vegetarianism. Careful consideration of them may have been the direct cause of your giving up meat; or they may be questions you are only vaguely becoming aware of. Either way, being a vegetarian inevitably involves thinking about the complex and often contentious implications of your choice. It is sometimes reassuring to recall that vegetarianism has a long and distinguished history. Whereas today meat is commonly abandoned on health grounds, in the past it was usually a reflection of a particular philosophical and ethical outlook.

An Attachment à la Plato

The vegetarian is an obvious figure of fun, and perhaps to some degree always has been. W. S. Gilbert, for instance, attributed vegetarian ideals to the Aesthete in *Patience,* and they were clearly intended to be laughed at as a pretentious folly:

> Then a sentimental passion of a vegetable
>   fashion must excite your languid spleen,
> An attachment *à la* Plato for a bashful young
>   potato, or a not-too-French French bean.
> Though the Philistines may jostle, you will
>   rank as an apostle in the high aesthetic band,
> If you walk down Piccadilly with a poppy or a
>   lily in your mediaeval hand.
> And everyone will say,

As you walk your flowery way,
'If he's content with a vegetable love which
   would certainly not suit *me*,
Why, what most particularly pure young man
   this pure young man must be!'

The earliest indication of vegetarianism as an integral part of a wider philosophical view is to be found in ancient Greece. It was Pythagoras, according to the Roman poet Ovid, who was the 'first to ban the serving of animal foods at our tables, first to express himself in such words as these . . . "O my fellow-men, do not defile your bodies with sinful foods . . . The earth affords a lavish supply of riches, of innocent foods, and offers you banquets that involve no bloodshed or slaughter."'

The Roman historian Plutarch (*c.* AD 46–*c.* 120) also referred back to the vegetarian beliefs of Pythagoras in graphic terms in his essay *On the Eating of Flesh:*

> Can you really ask what reason Pythagoras had for abstaining from flesh? For my part I rather wonder both by what accident and in what state of soul or mind the first man did so, touched his mouth to gore and brought his lips to the flesh of a dead creature, he who set forth tables of dead, stale bodies and ventured to call food and nourishment the parts that had a little before bellowed and cried, moved and lived. How could his eyes endure the slaughter when throats were slit and hides flayed and limbs torn from limb? How could his nose endure the stench? How was it that the pollution did not turn away his taste, which made contact with the sores of others and sucked juices and serums from mortal wounds?[2]

Plutarch's rhetorical questions are as valid today as when he first posed them to the carnivores of the first century. As for Plato, he and his master Socrates are usually considered to have been vegetarians, though, in spite of W. S. Gilbert, there is no direct evidence.

Leonardo

Leonardo da Vinci (1452–1519) has some claim to be the first modern vegetarian, though — like much else about him — the foundations of his belief in a meatless diet remain shrouded in uncertainty. 'He who does not value life does not deserve it,' he wrote; and, like

Plutarch, he condemned the terrible barbarism that eating meat necessarily involves: 'From countless numbers will be stolen their little children, and the throats of these shall be cut, and they shall be quartered most barbarously.' And yet this colossal, contradictory genius also designed an ingenious piece of equipment for roasting meat, and this sensitive, highly cultured humanist would coolly examine the fear-stricken faces of condemned criminals in a spirit of absolute artistic detachment!

Vegetarianism received theoretical support from the French essayist Montaigne and later from Jean Jacques Rousseau, neither of whom, however, were practising vegetarians, though both, like Sir Thomas More in *Utopia* (1516; English translation 1556), saw the ideal society as existing on a meatless diet. In the eighteenth century John Wesley and his brother Charles were fervent vegetarians; but it was not until the nineteenth century that vegetarianism acquired two outstandingly articulate champions — the poet and philosopher Shelley, and George Bernard Shaw.

Shelley and the 'Unnatural Diet'

Percy Bysshe Shelley (1792–1822) is sometimes associated with the image of the typical vegetarian male as an effete and effeminate young man; but this — fortunately for vegetarianism — is a Victorian fiction.

The falsification began with Mary Shelley, the poet's wife and author of *Frankenstein*, who was persuaded by the Shelley family to suppress those aspects of her late husband's life and character that would strike mid-Victorian England as being in any way immoral, blasphemous, or politically offensive, whilst in the next generation Shelley's daughter-in-law, Lady Jane Shelley, made it her life's work to establish what Shelley's biographer Richard Holmes has called 'an unimpeachable feminine and Victorian idealization of the poet'.

Modern research, mainly by Richard Holmes, has revealed an altogether more robust Shelley: hard, courageous, politically committed, learned, witty, and occasionally — though perhaps unintentionally — cruel. His vegetarianism was the result, not of a vague humanitarian impulse, but of a carefully thought out philosophical view.

Shelley's early espousal of vegetarianism was confirmed and strengthened by meeting J. F. Newton, vegetarian, naturist, and

Zoroastrian. In the long philosophical notes to *Queen Mab* (1813), Shelley describes his feelings about eating animal flesh:

> I hold that the depravity of the physical and moral nature of man originated in his unnatural habits of life . . . The allegory of Adam and Eve eating of the tree of evil, and entailing upon their posterity the wrath of God and the loss of everlasting life, entails of no other explanation than the disease and crime that have flowed from unnatural diet.

By 'unnatural diet' Shelley meant a meat diet. Following J. F. Newton, he even explained the myth of Prometheus, the youth who stole fire from heaven and was chained for this crime to Mount Caucasus, where a vulture continually devoured his liver, in terms of a change to a carnivorous diet:

> How plain a language is spoken by all this! Prometheus (who represents the human race) effected some great change in the condition of his nature, and applied fire to culinary purposes; thus inventing an expedient for screening from his disgust the horrors of the shambles [i.e. slaughterhouse]. From this moment his vitals were devoured by the vulture of disease. It consumed his being in every shape of its loathsome and infinite variety, inducing the soul-quelling sinkings of premature and violent death. All vice rose from the ruin of healthful innocence. Tyranny, superstition, commerce, and inequality were then first known, when reason vainly attempted to guide the wanderings of exacerbated passion.

This ingenious argument is full of the passion of a young idealist, and few would now wish to follow Shelley in ascribing all political and social ills to meat-eating; but modern research has hinted at a possible confirmation of Shelley's claim that the introduction of cooking, allied with the eating of animal flesh, is associated with the proliferation of certain diseases. Dr Barry Commoner, an American scientist, has postulated the existence of what he called 'culinary carcinogens', suggesting that cooking certain foods in specific ways can cause cancer. Compare Shelley's words on the consequences of Prometheus' application of fire for culinary purposes: 'From this moment his vitals were devoured by the vulture of disease.'

Dr Commoner discovered that well-cooked hamburgers and beef extract (the base for stock cubes) contain a substance called a mutagen

— one that reacts with DNA and causes changes in the way a cell reproduces itself. Most, though not all, mutagens are also cancer-inducing.

Beef tissue, and the stock that derives from it, do not, according to Dr Commoner, contain mutagens in any significant quantity until they are boiled: the more boiling they undergo, the more the mutagen count increases. Because it was the *cooking* of the beef, rather than the beef itself, that seemed to be the source of the mutagen, Commoner went on to investigate common cooking procedures. Quarter-pound portions of lean ground beef were cooked for varying amounts of time: ninety seconds (rare), three minutes (medium) and five and a half minutes (well done). Sure enough, the mutagen content of each hamburger differed significantly: the rare hamburger had only one part in a hundred million of mutagen; that of the well done hamburger was fourteen times greater.

Japanese researchers have also worked on mutagens. They found that meat and fish that were smoked or cooked at temperatures over 300°C (572°F) contained many more mutagens than the same food in an uncooked state, which perhaps explains why Icelanders, who eat large quantities of smoked fish and sea birds, have a high incidence of stomach cancer.

Dr Commoner did not condemn meat eating as such: he merely pointed out the dangers of certain culinary processes in relation to meat. But as these processes are largely confined to the preparation of flesh foods and fish it is clear that meat eaters are more at risk than vegetarians. In this at least Shelley's version of the Prometheus myth has a disturbing relevance to the dietary habits of our time.

George Bernard Shaw

'It seems to me, looking at myself,' remarked G. B. Shaw in typical style, 'that I am a remarkably superior person, when you compare me with other writers, journalists, and dramatists; and I am perfectly content to put this down to my abstinence from meat.'

Shaw is easily the most notorious, as well as the most vociferous, modern vegetarian. He gave up eating meat in 1881, after reading Shelley, and thereafter spoke of meat-eating as 'cannibalism with its heroic dish omitted'.[3]

He had three main objections to a carnivorous diet. First, he considered that animals were, in every sense, fellow creatures and that to slaughter and eat them was nothing less than an abomination. He was careful, though, to distinguish between killing for food and killing for other reasons — self-defence, for instance. His commitment to vegetarianism was tempered by realism: 'We see the Buddhist having his path swept before him lest he should tread on an insect and kill it; but we do not see what the Buddhist does when he catches a flea that has kept him awake for an hour.'

Second, he saw meat-eating as being socially harmful:

> It involves a prodigious slavery of men to animals. Cows and sheep, with their *valetaille* of accoucheurs, graziers, shepherds, slaughtermen, butchers, milkmaids, and so forth, absorb a mass of human labour that should be devoted to the breeding and care of human beings. Some day, I hope, we shall live on air, and get rid of all the sanitary preoccupations which are so unpleasantly aggravated by meat-eating.

Third, Shaw, like Shelley, related the diminution of health and strength to eating meat. He referred to international athletes who abstained from eating scorched corpses and pointed to the bull, one of the strongest of animals and a complete vegetarian. Indeed he saw as one of the disadvantages of vegetarianism the accumulation of energy that was difficult to dissipate under normal conditions: 'What I want', he wrote, 'is a job of work. Thinning a jungle for preference. But whitewashing will serve.'

With Shaw's vegetarianism went an abstention from alcohol and tobacco; 'I flatly declare', he said, 'that a man fed on whisky and dead bodies cannot do the finest work of which he is capable.' Shaw lived to be ninety-four on his vegetarian and alcohol-free diet, though he was careful to complement it with constant exercise. He also managed to combine his dietary principles with a cuisine that was very far from being primitive or dourly 'back to Nature'.

Late in life Shaw took liver extract to counteract a haemoglobin deficiency, which, when it became generally known, caused some consternation and anger among hard line vegetarians. In a letter to Symon Gould, founder of the American Vegetarian Party, that was published in the *American Vegetarian,* Shaw stoutly defended his apparent lapse in a strongly practical and pugnacious manner:

> Liver extract you would take if you developed pernicious anaemia.
> If you were diabetic you would take insulin. If you had oedema you

would take thyroid. You may think you wouldn't; but you would if your diet failed to cure you. You would try any of the gland extracts, the mineral drugs, the so-called vaccines, if it were that or your death.

Shaw's self-confidence is infectious and inspiring for any vegetarian, especially perhaps for those who have to follow their choice of diet in an unsympathetic environment. We all need our beliefs confirming from time to time; and when this happens there is no finer tonic than George Bernard Shaw's sublime egoism.

Dons, Dictators, and Cranks

Vegetarianism has certainly attracted its fair share of eccentrics, and undesirables. Affiliated to the former, though not himself a vegetarian, was the Revd C. L. Dodgson, of Christ Church, Oxford, otherwise known to the world as Lewis Carroll. Dodgson is of interest to the vegetarian because of his views on vivisection, as expressed in his pamphlet *Some Popular Fallacies About Vivisection*. On the proposition 'That man is infinitely more important than the lower animals, so that the infliction of animal suffering, however great, is justifiable if it prevent human suffering, however small' he commented:

> This fallacy can be assumed only when unexpressed. To put it into words is almost to refute it. Few, even in an age where selfishness has almost become a religion, dare openly avow a selfishness so hideous as this! While there are thousands, I believe, who would be ready to assure the vivisectors that, so far as their personal interests are concerned, they are ready to forego any prospect they may have of a diminution of pain, if it can only be secured by the infliction of so much pain on innocent creatures. [4]

As for the argument — which is still put forward whenever vegetarians and carnivores clash in debate — that human and animal suffering differ in kind, Dodgson deftly parried it with an appeal to the prevailing Darwinism. It is inconsistent, he says, to maintain, on the one hand, that 'man is twin-brother to the monkey' whilst holding, on the other hand, that both experience pain in a different way. 'Let them be at least consistent,' he concluded, 'and when they have proved that the lessening of the *human* suffering is an end so great and glorious as to justify any means that will secure it, let them give the anthropomorphid ape the benefit of the argument. Further than this I will not ask them to go, but will resign them in confidence to the guidance of an inexorable logic.'

The most infamously undesirable vegetarian is undoubtedly Adolf Hitler, who characteristically linked meat-eating with the decay of civilization. In this he believed he was following Wagner; but Wagner did not practise what he preached: for him, vegetarianism was for the perfect world, not for this one. Hitler's vegetarianism is certainly an embarrassment for the vegetarian cause: how can it be argued that meat-eating is capable of exerting an adverse effect on the moral nature when a man like Hitler spent a good deal of his life avoiding flesh foods? One can only suggest that it is the exception that proves the rule, and that the rights and wrongs of killing animals for food have nothing to do with the accident of Hitler's vegetarianism. Conversely, it would be absurd to argue that Hitler was what he was *because* of his vegetarianism.

Other, distinctly peripheral, advocates of a fleshless diet include the many sects and minority cults that have embraced vegetarianism as a radical alternative to the acquisitive, exploitive world around them — from the Doukhobors, who, fired with the high ideals of Tolstoy, migrated from Czarist Russia to the wide wheatlands of Canada to practise their ascetic brand of vegetarianism and organize nude protest marches, to the hippies of Haight Ashbury.

Today there are vegetarians prominent in nearly every area of public life — from politicians, writers and artists, to sports personalities and showbusiness stars. A few examples from an extensive listing published by the *Vegetarian Times* in America in December 1984 follows:

Showbusiness:	*Music:*	*Authors:*
Julie Christie	Jeff Beck	Piers Anthony
Peter Cushing	Kate Bush	Brigid Brophy
Sandy Dennis	Johnny Cash	Hans Holzer
Samantha Eggar	David Cassidy	R. D. Laing
Patrick Macnee	Chubby Checker	Frances Moore
Pamela Sue Martin	Jimmy Cliff	Lappé
Hayley Mills	Ray and Dave	Malcolm
William Shatner	Davies (The Kinks)	Muggeridge

Showbusiness:	*Music:*	*Authors:*
Terence Stamp	Donovan	Helen Nearing
Twiggy	Peter Gabriel	Isaac Singer
Dennis Weaver	Eddy Grant	
	George Harrison	
	Chrissie Hynde	
	Michael Jackson	
	Annie Lennox	
	Paul and Linda	
	McCartney	
	Todd Rungren	
	Rick Springfield	

There are many others — including Uri Geller and Bernard Weatherill, Speaker of the House of Commons. Amongst the many sportspersons who are vegetarians, the *Vegetarian Times* article features Andreas Cahling, a world class bodybuilder who became an ovo-lacto vegetarian to improve his health. As the caption to an impressive picture of Cahling in all his muscular glory says: 'His regimen of nuts, grains, vegetables, fruits and eggs is a far cry from the diet of most of his colleagues. In addition to meat and fish, Cahling cut out the protein powders and glandular extracts so commonly used by bodybuilders.'

What do all these people have in common — from Pythagoras, Shelley, and Shaw to Twiggy and Michael Jackson? Quite simply, each one of them, for a variety of reasons has decided to break the mould of a monolithic dietary system based on suffering and slaughter and opt for a more humane, and a healthier, alternative. For them, and for millions like them all around the world, the meat myth has been exploded. They have seen that eating meat is *not* essential to human life, but that it *is* a continuing and obscene affront both to human dignity and to the dignity of non-human animals.

But how justified are we in speaking of animals in this way? What are the grounds for the basic vegetarian belief that animals *have* rights that must be respected? To answer these questions we must examine the ethics of the vegetarian choice.

2.

THE ETHICAL DIET

> The [Cartesian] scientists administered beatings to dogs with perfect indifference and made fun of those who pitied the creatures as if they felt pain. They said the animals were clocks; that the cries they emitted when struck were only the noise of a little spring that had been touched, but that the whole body was without feeling. They nailed the poor animals up on boards by their four paws to vivisect them to see the circulation of the blood which was then a great subject of controversy.

THESE words were written by an unknown contemporary of the French philosopher René Descartes (1596–1650), whose world-view was encapsulated in the famous phrase *Cogito, ergo sum*: 'I think, therefore I am'. Man, in this view, is dignified by the process of thought; consciousness exalts him above the animal, vegetable, and mineral kingdoms, the members of which are, in a profoundly literal sense, 'thoughtless'.

For Descartes, animals have no awareness of either pleasure or pain, or indeed of any sensation or experience. They are simply *automata*, mechanical brutes, devoid of consciousness: 'It is nature which acts in them according to the disposition of their organs, just as a clock, which is only composed of wheels and weights, is able to measure the time more correctly than we can with all our wisdom.'

Today the Cartesian denial of consciousness to animals seems absurd, perhaps even obscene, on grounds of common sense alone. As Tom Regan has observed: 'The role of appeals to common sense . . . is not to guarantee the truth or reasonableness of a given belief, but to put the burden of proof on those who would deny it . . .'

The philosophical debate on this and other ethical issues is complex, and may seem irrelevant for most 'ordinary' vegetarians. But in fact a basic knowledge of the ethical implications of the vegetarian choice is both interesting in itself and necessary if we are to convince others that our views deserve serious consideration. The cause of vegetarianism is not advanced by example alone, no matter how many stars decide to give up meat. Progress is made through social pressure and, at the individual level, by argument and debate, the starting point for which must be the ethical basis of vegetarianism.

This can be reduced to a simple premise: that animals are sentient, conscious creatures, with the power to distinguish between pleasure and pain. It is not only an assumption made by vegetarians and vegans: thousands of animal owners, who are probably also meat eaters, would certainly agree with this; and yet, every year, over 200 million cattle and calves are slaughtered for food, whilst the total number of animal deaths for this purpose is probably incalculable.

To justify ethically slaughter on this scale it is necessary to deny, as Descartes did, that animals are capable of suffering, or to try and minimize their sufferings by claiming that they experience pain in a different way, or in a different degree, from human beings. Neither position is easy to defend. Animals — for all Descartes' arguments — *are* sentient creatures; to treat them as such is to acknowledge a fundamental ethical relationship between animals and us.

It cannot be finally *proved* that animals feel pain, though they certainly act *as if* they do; but then I cannot be sure that the person whose toe I accidentally tread on is sentient in this respect: he too may be acting *as if* he felt pain. Of course he can express himself forcibly in language, whereas an animal can only struggle or scream; but I have no way of knowing whether the pain he feels is the same sensation of hurt and annoyance I experience when someone treads on *my* toe. The point is that I give him the benefit of the doubt; I acknowledge his discomfort because he signals to me in ways I can instinctively understand that he is suffering. Moreover, I expect other people to understand *me* when I suffer.

We give animals no such benefit. Whilst it may be difficult to argue that animals are aware of the concepts of life and death — for instance, that the existence of the one presupposes, from common experience, the inevitability of the other — it seems safe to presume that they have an instinctive desire to preserve their own life. That indeed is their principal daily aim and the motive force of the evolutionary process. A fox fleeing the hounds may not have a clear idea what constitutes death, or what succeeds the extinction of his breath, but he knows it is a thing to be avoided for as long as possible and acts accordingly.

The killing of an animal for food is thus the ultimate violation of its most basic desire: to stay alive. But the violation does not stop there. As well as being killed, animals are made to suffer both before and during the killing process: they are bred to an unnatural death. In a typical veal house calves are reared in narrow crates, unable to exercise or even turn round, and often in the dark. The calves are commonly tied by the neck in such crates for the duration of their short lives. Because the floors of the crates are slatted, the joints of the animals' legs become malformed, and many are unable to stand properly or walk when taken out of their crates for slaughtering. They are fed on an all-liquid diet that is low in iron to give an unnatural white colour to the meat. Thus they suffer from anaemia. They are also denied the fibre that all ruminants need, so that they are often forced to gnaw their wooden crates and as a result develop bowel disorders. Finally, they are denied water, which forces them to drink a milk substitute that increases their liveweight gain.

It has been said many times that if we all had to kill our own meat we should all be vegetarians. Certainly few meat-eaters give the actual killing process any thought, and even fewer would willingly witness the everyday activities of their local slaughterhouse. Most carnivores seem to cherish the belief that the animals they eat have died without suffering or trauma; but this is hardly the case. One system for despatching chickens involves the fattened birds being hung on a conveyor line which passes over a trough of electrically charged water, into which the birds' heads are dipped to stun them. They are then fed into the rails of the slaughtering machine itself, where a rotating saw bleeds them to death, if they are lucky, by cutting their throats and main arteries. A secondary mechanism deals with any that manage to survive the first one. Their heads then pass through a decapitator, which stretches their necks until they tear. In the final stage the chickens are automatically gutted and washed prior to sorting and packing.

Actually, chickens killed in this way should think themselves lucky.

A typical veal house in the UK showing the narrow crates in which the calves are reared all their lives, unable to exercise or turn round, and often in the dark. When nearing slaughter weight, the calves fill the crates. *(Photographs: Compassion in World Farming)*

In many parts of America the brutally inefficient poleaxe is still in use. This is really a sledgehammer rather than an axe. It has a long handle and the intention is to knock the beast unconscious with a single blow. With a moving target this calls for almost impossible precision, and if the swing is a fraction astray the hammer can crash through the animal's eye or nose; several more blows may be needed as the animal thrashes around in pain and terror.

It's not just the patent cruelty of the rearing, transportation and killing of animals that people are now so concerned about. Animals are perfectly capable of feeling the terror of impending death — as capable as you or I. Pigs are particularly sensitive and vulnerable to stress. They can literally die of fright. Their flesh, when they are terrified in the slaughterhouse, becomes pale, soft, and what is termed 'exudative'. Even before they reach the killing line the risk of death is high. There is a name for this condition: Porcine Stress Syndrome, the symptoms of which are extreme stress, rigidity, blotchy skin, panting, anxiety, and often sudden death. In such a state the pig's flesh becomes flooded with toxins, which are later consumed by humans — uric acid, for instance, which can predispose humans towards kidney stones, gout, and arthritis.

Even if we were to fulfil our minimum obligation towards animals and minimize the distress and pain of both the rearing and slaughtering processes, it still does not bestow the absolute right to kill them for food. This has been classically argued by Brigid Brophy. It is certain that I do not have the right to kill anyone I choose — however painlessly — just because I happen to like the flavour of their flesh; it is equally certain that I am not in a position to judge whether the life of the person I have chosen for my meal is worth more to him, or her, than the animal's is to it. If anything the human's life is worth less, since, unlike the animal, the human has the unique capability of voluntarily depriving himself of life by committing suicide. The only safe course, morally speaking, is to assume a parity of value for life in any given creature, be it human or otherwise.

Vivisection
In pleading the case for the rights of animals one runs smack up against formidable moral problems in those cases where there is a direct clash between the vital interests of humans and animals; most acutely, on the question of vivisection.

To hold that vivisection is never justified under any circumstances is as hard to justify as the opposite belief. Like people who go out of their way to rescue ill-treated donkeys, or who save kittens from drowning, or go to extraordinary lengths to save the life of any animal, the vegetarian runs a high risk of being accused that his or her priorities are wrong. Animals, the common argument runs, are being held in more esteem than human beings. Vegetarianism and vivisection are intimately related issues, and every vegetarian must be prepared to be confronted at some time or other on the question of experiments on live animals. Brigid Brophy provides one possible response:

> I can see nothing (except our being able to get away with it) which lets us pick on animals that would not equally let us pick on idiot humans (who would be more useful) or, for the matter of that, on a few humans of any sort whom we might sacrifice for the good of the many.[1]

It is, in any case, perfectly possible to feel compassion for both human beings and animals; it is not a case of mutually exclusive options, for on a global scale the adoption of a predominantly vegetarian diet would have considerable benefits for the majority of the human race (see Chapter 4). Growing crops to feed to animals, who are then slaughtered to provide human beings with protein that is freely available from other sources, is a hopelessly inefficient system. On average, about 90 per cent of the protein in the plant foods that are fed to animals is used by the animals themselves, leaving only about 10 per cent of the original protein value for those who eat their flesh. Ending this stupendous wastage and turning over land now used to grow animal feed to the cultivation of crops for direct human consumption would add immeasurably to the sum of human happiness.

But even if this were not true, the obvious answer to the charge that vegetarians and anti-vivisectionists are anthropomorphizing and sentimentalizing animals, and lavishing their sympathy on inferior species, lies precisely in the fact that animals *are* inferior to the will and intelligence of human beings. Brigid Brophy again:

> The whole case for behaving decently to animals rests on the fact that we are the superior species. We are the species uniquely capable of imagination, rationality and moral choice — and that is precisely

why we are under the obligation to recognize and respect the rights
of animals.

Animal experimentation is now an important political issue, so
important to some people that they have adopted the wholly
unjustifiable option of violence and terrorism. But even the majority
of moderate supporters of animal rights, who rightly disassociate
themselves from the policies of the extremists, feel frustrated at the
painfully slow progress that is being made in reducing the number
of animal experiments. Of the experiments themselves, little need
be said here. They range from deliberate poisoning and the
administering of electric shocks, to forced consumption of alcohol
and tobacco, the testing of cosmetics, and the hideous practice of
parabiosis (sewing two animals together).

For the ethical vegetarian, then, two things are clear: first, that animals
have an innate will to live and a corresponding desire not to die; second,
that animals suffer both in the rearing process and in the slaughtering
methods of modern meat production.

There is a further ground for ethical vegetarianism: the idea of
species relationship. Animals are our fellow creatures, inferior to us
in several important ways, but also superior to us in others — for
instance, strength, stamina, sensitivity to the natural environment,
and so on. This recognition implicitly refutes the arrogance of
speciesism that we have an absolute, inalienable right to dispose of
other species as we see fit because our own is the most intellectually
developed.

The ethical view is that we owe our fellow creatures a basic sense
of kinship, which acknowledges an obligation not to cause them
unnecessary pain or death. Ironically, this kinship could be used to
argue in favour of vivisection: for instance, if certain animals were
not so similar to us in specific physiological details they could be
of no possible use in medical research. One cannot therefore argue
in favour of using rats in medical experiments, with the aim of
improving the human lot, as well as dismissing the idea of kinship
with animals.

This seems clear enough. But there are several powerful and frequently voiced arguments against the case for ethical vegetarianism.

The first is that killing for food is 'natural' — i.e. it is part of the given order of things. Animals kill each other to stay alive; so why shouldn't humans kill animals — given that man is, in the view of ethical vegetarianism, a fellow animal? If it is not wrong for a fox to kill a rabbit for food, why is it wrong for a man to kill a sheep, or a cow, or a pig?

It is certainly true that the balance of Nature depends on a highly complex and sensitive relationship between hunters and hunted. But this finely tuned predatory system is very different from modern animal husbandry. More importantly, the argument that the killing in nature of the members of one species by those of another does not justify the practice of intensive farming: it justifies the practice of hunting for food. The fox does not breed rabbits for his own consumption, or keep them, from birth to death, in an environment of his own making. He hunts them on a one-to-one basis when hunger dictates that he should do so. Certainly killing takes place in Nature; indeed it is a vital mechanism. But it is the usual consequence of hunting, not of mass exploitation. It would be difficult for a vegetarian to argue that eating meat was unethical if carnivores had to go out every day to stalk their prey, creature to creature; for, in this case, the human is functioning in exactly the same way as the fox or the lion.

And yet we have been arguing that all animals have a right to life, and this must include the victims of animal predators, whose right to life is not diminished or modified according to which particular species is intent on killing them. How can the vegetarian respond to this paradox?

Principally, by distinguishing between killing for necessity and killing for whim. The animal predator has no choice in the matter: Nature, in the form of instinct and biological functioning, dictates the manner in which food is to be obtained, as well as the specific types of food to be hunted. Moreover, predators are careful to take only the minimum needed to fill their needs: they do not systematically slaughter the entire population of their prey species, for to do so would be to eliminate their main source of food.

For humans, however, these considerations do not apply. An animal in the wild has no choice: a human being does. For the animal, killing food is necessary; for the human it is not.

The second argument commonly urged in justification of eating meat is that animals are not our equals and that it therefore follows that we cannot apply the same moral standards to them as we do to other human beings. We have already seen the extreme development of this position in the ideas of Descartes. The philosopher David Hume (1711-76) also expressed the idea of human superiority over animals, maintaining that our relationship with them consists at bottom of 'absolute command on one side, and servile obedience on the other . . . Our permission is the only tenure, by which they hold their possessions'. As Keith Akers has pointed out: 'The problem with this theory is that it justifies too much . . . Hume's arguments appear to justify not only colonialization and sexual discrimination, but probably also racism, infanticide, and basically anything one can get away with.'[2]

Pushing this argument to its logical conclusion, we could have no objection if extra-terrestrial invaders of a higher intelligence than us were to land on Earth and decide to take us as their natural prey species, on the ground that we were, in their eyes, altogether unfitted to be treated as their equals.

The speciesist view has an ancient lineage. Chrysippus, a Greek Stoic philosopher of the third century BC, regarded animals as having been created solely for the use of man. According to Cicero, in the *De Natura Deorum*, he held that the soul 'is given to the pig as a kind of salt, to keep it from rotting'. In the Middle Ages the Catholic philosopher and theologian Thomas Aquinas (*c.* 1225-74), in his *Summa Theologica*, excluded the animal kingdom from ethical consideration on the grounds that animals lacked the faculty of reason. But this is far from certain the more we learn of animal behaviour. Speaking purely from common sense, Jeremy Bentham (1748-1832), the political economist and prophet of Utilitarianism (the doctrine that 'It is the greatest happiness of the greatest number that is the measure of right and wrong'), observed:

> A full-grown horse or dog is beyond comparison a more rational, as well as a more conversable animal, than an infant of a day, or a week, or even a month, old. But suppose the case were otherwise, what would it avail? The question is not, Can they *reason?* nor, Can they *talk* but, Can they *suffer?*[3]

Ethical vegetarianism, then, does not insist that humans and animals are the same in every respect; but that the differences between them are not great enough to deny animals basic moral consideration. Whilst it is necessary to recognize the differences between human and non-human animals, and thus to distinguish to some degree between the rights of each, it does not follow that the principle of equality in nature should apply only to humans. Men and women should be treated equally, but not to the extent that they should be given rights they do not require. An example given by Peter Singer is the demand by some feminists that women should be allowed the right to have abortions on demand. Because they are campaigning for equality between men and women, does it therefore mean that they must logically argue in favour of men receiving abortions on demand? Of course not: that is an absurdity. The point is, as Singer goes on to express it:

> The extension of the basic principle of equality from one group to another does not imply that we must treat both groups in exactly the same way, or grant exactly the same rights to both groups . . . The basic principle of equality does not require equal or identical *treatment*; it requires equal *consideration*. [4]

The third common objection to vegetarianism is to push the refusal to take life for food to the point of absurdity. This is a familiar ploy, and every vegetarian encounters it. The argument runs as follows: it is wrong to kill animals for food; animals are living creatures; therefore it is wrong to kill any living thing for food; therefore it is wrong to 'kill' plants and vegetables by removing them from their natural environment and eating them. If this is not so, then it is not wrong to kill animals for food.

This seems logical enough on the face of it, and put forcefully it can throw the new vegetarian unaccustomed to dealing with confirmed carnivores in debate. This particular argument seems to find support in the philosophy of fruitarianism, for fruitarians eat nothing but fruit, nuts, or seeds — i.e. those natural products that can be eaten without injuring or destroying any animal or plant.

There is, though, an ethical distinction between plants and animals based on physiological considerations. You will read that plants feel pain, that they respond to music, that they 'scream' when a leaf is torn off; that they can read people's minds; but there is no solid evidence to back up the notion of plants as sentient creatures in the same way as an animal clearly is. Pain is a key factor in the survival ability of organisms with central nervous systems and mobility. Plants have neither a central nervous system, nor mobility: an animal needs the ability to feel pain in order to survive; a lettuce does not.

The infliction of pain may seem an obvious, indeed a fundamental consideration in our relations with animals; but this has been questioned by the philosopher R. G. Frey in his book *Rights, Killing and Suffering: Moral Vegetarianism and Applied Ethics,* which is principally a refutation of the arguments for vegetarianism put forward by Peter Singer in *Animal Liberation.* Frey argues that the pain and suffering experienced by animals whilst being reared and killed for food is not sufficient reason to stop eating them. He argues his case on three main fronts: (1) that the total adoption of vegetarianism would not result in an overall increase of pleasure over pain, for a variety of reasons — for instance, the loss of jobs associated with meat production; (2) that vegetarianism is actually an ineffective way to reduce the pain and suffering experienced by farm animals: no one abstention from eating meat will have any effect on the total demand for meat; and (3) that there is no need to give up eating meat in order to lobby for change, since it is not *we* who engage in the cruel practices inevitable in the production of meat.

Frey rejects arguments for vegetarianism that depend on the moral rights of animals; pain *is* a consideration, but only to the extent that we should be concerned to devise painless ways of killing animals. But as one reviewer of Frey's book observed: 'Such an approach ignores the fact that many vegetarians are influenced by a recognition of capacities in animals which parallel those in human beings, on the basis of which we respect their lives and consider it inappropriate to use them merely as instruments of our own pleasures, particularly when these pleasures are restricted to the production of a limited range of gastronomic sensations.'[5]

This brings us back to Bentham, whose emphasis on the capacity for suffering as, in Singer's words, 'the vital characteristic that gives a being the right to equal consideration' is the keystone of any argument in support of animal rights:

If a being suffers there can be no moral justification for refusing to take that suffering into consideration. No matter what the nature of the being, the principle of equality requires that its suffering be counted equally with the like suffering — in so far as rough comparisons can be made — of any other being. If a being is not capable of suffering, or of experiencing enjoyment or happiness, there is nothing to be taken into account. So the limit of sentience (using the term as a convenient if not strictly accurate shorthand for the capacity to suffer and/or experience enjoyment) is the only defensible boundary of concern for the interests of others. To mark this boundary by some other characteristic like intelligence or rationality would be to mark it in an arbitrary manner. Why not choose some other characteristic, like skin colour?[5]

But how can we be absolutely sure that plants don't suffer? Is it beyond dispute that plants are not sentient?

This is a subtle objection to vegetarianism, and again it is commonly encountered. Some people raise it in good faith, as a result of a deep concern for the sanctity of life in any form. Usually, however, one hears it put forward by people who have no such concern. It is used in an attempt to show the impossibility of adopting an ethical position in regard to food; if plants can be shown to suffer, the only logical course is to stop eating them. If this is not done, then the vegetarian may as well resume eating animals as well.

We have already seen that there is no evolutionary reason for plants to feel pain, any more than stones or water. Science — as opposed to fringe researchers relying on 'psychic attunement' — has found no grounds for believing otherwise. A plant has nothing that resembles a central nervous system, and there is nothing in the observable behaviour of a plant that suggests the capacity to feel pain — to suffer. In short, the belief that plants feel pain is, on present evidence, unjustified; but even if this was not so, as Peter Singer has shown, it must still be true that plants suffer less than animals, with their far more advanced physiologies, and so we should be bound to choose the lesser evil and eat those things that suffer least.

Veganism

At this point it will be as well to say something about veganism, which, like vegetarianism, is attracting a growing number of followers.

Veganism, which some see as 'real' vegetarianism, is far more than a dietary system. It is, according to the UK Vegan Society,

> a way of living on the products of the plant kingdom to the exclusion of flesh, fish, fowl, eggs, animal milk and its derivatives (the taking of honey being left to individual conscience). It encourages the study and use of alternatives for all commodities normally derived wholly or partly from animals.
>
> The objects of The Vegan Society are to further knowledge of, and interest in, sound nutrition and in the vegan method of agriculture and food production as a means of increasing the potential of the earth to the physical, moral and economic advantage of mankind.[6]

More succinctly, Eva Batt, a former Secretary of the Vegan Society, expresses the broad context within which veganism operates: 'Veganism is one thing and one thing only — a way of living which avoids exploitation, whether it be of our fellow men, the animal population, or the soil upon which we rely for our existence.'

The vegan therefore eats no animal derivatives, and this prohibition can extend to non-edible products such as leather, silk, wool, and ivory, as well as to activities such as horse racing and circus acts involving animals.

Reverence for life — compassion — is thus the very heart of veganism and allies it with similar approaches in philosophy and religion. Albert Schweitzer, though not a vegan himself, stated the position clearly: 'Ethics consist in this, that I experience the necessity of practising the same reverence for life toward all will-to-live, as toward my own.' And of flesh-eating Schweitzer wrote that it was not in accordance with the finer feelings: 'It belongs to the characteristics of Man to be kind and compassionate to all creatures . . . I am convinced that the destiny of Man is, to become more and more humane.'

This all too often seems like a dream: humans appear incapable of sustaining a sense of reverence in relation to the lives of other human beings, let alone to those of animals. But the idea of reverence for life is a persistent one in human culture and may yet lead to the Utopia of which Schweitzer dreamed.

Gandhi, too, was concerned with the idea of what in Hinduism is called *ahimsa* — 'dynamic harmlessness':

> The only means for realization of Truth is *Ahimsa* . . . [It] is not the

crude thing it has been made to appear. Not to hurt any living thing is no doubt a part of *Ahimsa*, but it is its least expression. The principle of *Ahimsa* is hurt by every evil thought, by undue haste, by lying, by hatred, by wishing ill to anybody.[7]

In Jainism, *ahimsa* is accorded a central place. The first of the Five Great Vows taken by a Jain monk is: 'I renounce all killing of living beings . . . Nor shall I myself kill living beings or cause others to do it, nor consent to it . . .'.[8] Jainism seems an impossibly perfectionist religion, yet its fundamental outlook is ethically — even logically — unassailable:

> All living beings love their life, desire pleasure, and are averse to pain; they dislike any injury to themselves; everybody is desirous of life, and to every being, his own life is very dear.

This is not the place to consider the philosophical and ethical pros and cons of veganism as against vegetarianism. There have been times in the past when relations between the two camps were frosty; but outright antagonism is now less common. Many vegetarians follow their commitment through to the logical conclusion of veganism; others remain, in the eyes of more militant vegans, uncommitted and dilettante. But these are issues on which it is impossible to dogmatize. Freedom is indivisible — the freedom to eat meat, to abstain from meat, or to avoid all exploitation of living creatures: all these freedoms, in the end, must be respected. This does not mean that we cannot try and persuade, argue, even cajole others into accepting our views; but we cannot insist on a particular dietary system for everyone. And what applies to meat-eaters from the vegetarian point of view applies to vegetarians from the vegan. We must be content that, as the years pass, more people are feeling the justice of the arguments in favour of vegetarianism and animal rights, and that there does indeed seem to be a gradual, though at times painfully slow, evolution towards a more humane relationship with non-human animals, as well as a more responsible attitude to the Earth itself. The same kind of general evolutionary drift may be true of vegetarianism as well. As Victoria Moran has observed: 'most of the serious ethical vegetarians I know think of themselves as not being vegan *yet*'. In any case, it is more important as things now stand to have taken the first step away from the consumption of animal flesh, no matter how small and ineffectual that step may seem, than to have leaped straight into veganism and active agitation against animal oppression. This point was made by Peter Singer:

> Vegans, then, are right to say that we ought not to use dairy products. They are living demonstrations of the practicality and nutritional soundness of a diet that is totally free from the exploitation of other animals. At the same time, it should be said that, in our present speciesist world, it is not easy to keep so strictly to what is morally right. Most people have difficulty enough taking the step to vegetarianism: if asked to give up milk and cheese at the same time they could be so alarmed that they end up doing nothing at all. A reasonable and defensible plan of action is to tackle the worst abuses first . . . animal flesh and factory farm eggs . . . While someone who gave up animal flesh and simply replaced it with an increased amount of cheese would not really be doing very much for animals, anyone who replaces animal flesh with vegetable protein, while continuing to eat milk products occasionally, has made a major step toward the liberation of animals.[9]

In Chapter 1 we briefly mentioned the vegetarian beliefs of the ancient Greeks and Romans. These ancient vegetarian philosophers upheld their views that it was wrong to eat animals on several grounds: a belief in a mythical vegetarian golden age, when man, in a state of primeval innocence and virtue, lived in harmony with animals; a belief in the transmigration of souls, which meant that animals either had been or would be human beings; medical concern that eating meat was injurious to the health of the body, or a related religious concern that it was harmful to the soul; and what is now the core of modern ethical vegetarianism — compassion for the suffering experienced by animals that are killed for food.

The contemporary philosophical debate about vegetarianism began in earnest in the 1970s, though its modern roots go back to the nineteenth century; but neither the debate itself nor the plurality of views it has produced are new. The situation was paralleled in ancient Greece, in the disparate philosophical views on vegetarianism held by such as Pythagoras, Plutarch, Empedocles, Theophrastus, Plotinus, and Porphyry. It is precisely because of this historical link that, according to Daniel Dombrowski, 'the contemporary opponent to philosophical vegetarianism may come to realize that the position he opposes cannot be dismissed merely as a fad or as a narrow, sectarian position'. [10]

Modern ethical vegetarianism also owes a debt to Charles Darwin, who, like Jeremy Bentham, provided philosophical weight to the conviction that animals deserve our respect whilst failing to take personal note of his own conclusions. Darwin's theory of evolution emphasized that 'there is no fundamental difference between man and the higher mammals'. Dombrowski summarizes the implications of this as follows:

> Animals feel pain, love, have the desire to be loved, suffer from ennui, have dreams, and for all we know, may be self-conscious as well as conscious. Although animals do not have the ennobling belief in God, many human beings do not have this belief either (nor do some men have reason), and we do not (or should not) kill and eat *them* ... Once the weight of evidence in favour of Darwin's theory became apparent, practically every earlier justification of man's supreme place in creation and his dominion over the animals had to be rejected. Darwin signals a revolution in our perception of animals: we *are* animals! [11]

It was said by Henry Salt, an Eton housemaster who was one of the first modern champions of vegetarianism, in his pamphlet *The Logic of Vegetarianism* that success in what he termed 'the reform of diet' depended on 'a sincere belief in the moral rightness of the cause'. His point was that all the arguments in favour of vegetarianism in the end reflect a fundamental ethical position, and it is this that gives the logic of vegetarianism its force. 'The *spirit* in which one takes up vegetarianism', Salt concluded, 'is the main factor in the result. It is useless to look for any absolute proof in such matters — the proof is in one's self — for those, at least, who have heart to feel, and brain to ponder, the cruelty and folly of flesh-eating. It is an issue where logic is as wholly on the one side as habit is wholly on the other, and where habit is as certainly the shield of barbarism as logic is the sword of humaneness.'

3.

STAYING ALIVE

THE ethical arguments for adopting a vegetarian diet are compelling. They are also contentious, and academically fashionable. Professional philosophers have begun to colonize the subject, and even the 'ordinary' vegetarian is urging the moral force and logic of the ethical case almost as a matter of course. But in the end, a debate on ethical grounds can often turn into a mere confrontation of *opinion*. There is also a danger that the ethical arguments can become elevated into the *only* reason for abstention from meat-eating. It is possible for the ethical vegetarian to become dismissive of those who give up meat for the 'wrong' reasons — on health grounds, for instance, or simply because meat is too expensive. The consequence is a rigid emphasis on activism and commitment, when flexibility and pragmatism are what is really needed.

Ironically, the medical and nutritional Establishment, reacting to scientific data, are poised to do more for animal welfare than all the activists and well-meaning theorists put together. In 1979 the *British Medical Journal*'s 'Prescription for a Better British Diet' recommended a reduction of meat consumption by 15 per cent, whilst in 1983 *The Lancet* called for a 25 per cent reduction. Calls such as these have real impact in the long term and are already materially affecting national eating habits. The UK meat industry is also feeling the pinch from other, more oblique, directions. For instance, *The Vegetarian*, in 1984, reported how the executive officer of the Smithfield Market Tenants Association was being harassed on two fronts — 'the vegetarians and the [Greater London Council], whose proposed restrictions on heavy lorries in London streets threatened business at Smithfield Market. He views the GLC's plans as "even more detrimental to the market than some of the vegetarian theorists who currently infest the capital".'

When we turn from ethical theory and philosophy to questions of health and nutritional sufficiency in relation to a meatless diet we are back in the world of facts. We have to concern ourselves with hard data and physical realities, not philosophical abstractions, however important they may be. The health and nutritional issues, indeed, are for many people the *fundamental* issues: they are matters of common, daily concern, which may or may not assume equal importance with ethical or ecological considerations.

It is now commonplace, even in orthodox nutritional circles, that the typical diet of the developed world is both nutritionally deficient and productive of immense health problems, some of which we shall be looking at later in this chapter. At the centre of such a diet is meat, high in protein, but also high in fat, and lacking in the dietary fibre we now know to be essential for good health.

Meat is not the only villain of the piece. Highly refined convenience foods, with their insidious and often unnecessary additives, also play a key part in the declining health profile of the developed world. In conjunction with the potential dangers of meat-eating such foods can become, literally, lethal. At the same time, the vegetarian alternative is being taken up by millions worldwide. By 1984, according to a Gallup survey, one in five Britons had reduced their consumption of meat and there is now a definite trend in the UK towards a vegetarian diet. The *Daily Telegraph*, reporting the survey, said: 'The conscious avoidance of meat and outright vegetarianism has increased by around 60 per cent in the last year, according to Mr Gregory Sams, chairman of Realeat, which sold more than seven million non-meat burgers last year [1983]. Avoidance is most pronounced among the 16 to 24 age group.' Even in Australia — land of the meat-eater par excellence — things are changing. In the four years to 1981–2, beef and veal consumption dropped from 67.5 to 49.2kg per person per year, and the trend is continuing.

Vegetarianism, then, is no longer a minority 'fad', but a global development. Nor is it possible to delineate a stereotype for the modern vegetarian, who is now likely to come from almost any walk of life. The new vegetarian is also much better informed than his predecessors generally were about the key issues relating to a non-meat diet: he or she will certainly be aware of the dangers of refined, additive-laden foods, as well as of the ethical and ecological aspects of the vegetarian case. There is also a new breed: those who are not yet ready to commit themselves, and perhaps their families, to vegetarianism proper, but who are sufficiently aware of the health and nutrition facts to want to reduce their meat intake and their dependence on processed foods.

Starting Out

Becoming a vegetarian, from a practical point of view, may seem theoretically easy. Obviously, one simply gives up eating flesh foods. But how should this be done? Should you wake up on a Monday morning and decide that from now on you will never eat meat again, or should you try to adapt to a meatless diet gradually?

Vegetarians from birth — of which there are a growing number — clearly have no problems in this respect; their diet is settled and natural to them. But those who take up vegetarianism in early adulthood, or even in middle age, do need to ease themselves into their new dietary system in easy stages and give themselves time to adjust, both physically and psychologically, to this new way of eating.

Begin by replacing meat meals with simple vegetarian dishes using familiar ingredients (the recipes at the end of the book are ideal for this purpose); then slowly increase the weekly ratio of vegetarian meals over meat-based ones. Don't worry for the moment that you may be consuming prohibited substances outside the home — for instance, pastry containing animal fat, or food products containing gelatin or suet. A detailed knowledge of what you can and cannot legitimately eat as a vegetarian only comes with time. For the moment, be content with phasing out such staple flesh foods as pork, beef, lamb, ham, chicken, bacon, etc., from your diet. Once you have conquered the idea of meat as the linchpin of your diet, the rest is comparatively easy.

At the same time, and preferably before you begin to eliminate meat completely, you should familiarize yourself with some basic nutritional facts. A common criticism of vegetarianism is that it requires a degree in nutritional science to avoid dangerous deficiencies of essential nutrients. This is another hoary old myth; but it is true, however, that a minimum amount of basic information on the nutritional make-up of a well-balanced vegetarian diet is necessary (the same in fact applies to meat-eaters and *their* diet). As a general rule of thumb, don't restrict your diet to only one or two foods — e.g. cheese and potatoes, rice and beans. Variety is the simple key to sound nutrition, and if you are going straight from meat-eating to veganism it is even more important not to rely on a limited number of foods.

Some people, though, particularly those who have decided on ethical grounds that they cannot go on eating animal flesh, will find the gradualist approach inappropriate or unacceptable. Their convictions will demand an immediate change of diet. For them, the best and safest way to bring this about is to plan the changeover in detail by drawing up a full week's menu that is followed to the letter. There is no shortage of books on which to base such a plan (see the Reading List for a selection), and in the UK the Vegetarian Society will be glad to help with any queries you may have.

My own experience was of a gradual abstention from meat. Over a period of about six months my meat consumption was reduced drastically, but painlessly, by my wife, who was already a vegetarian. Then one day I realized that I could not face the steaming Shepherd's Pie (hitherto an object of intense craving) that had been placed before me. My career as a carnivore was over.

It is not this easy for everyone. Many experience desperate withdrawal symptoms after giving up meat, and some vegetarians retain particular longings for years. In my case, the smell of bacon cooking tempted me for some months after becoming a full-time vegetarian, though its grip on me is now happily relaxed.

Some will experience more severe reactions than I did — not only cravings for particular meat dishes, but also physical symptoms, such as lassitude, or even psychological reactions, such as depression. As one American vegetarian put it, 'Giving up steak and chops in the United States is like becoming an atheist in the Vatican City' — a sentiment all new vegetarians, whether Americans or not, can sympathize with. When you become a vegetarian, and people begin to be aware of the fact, there are many social adjustments to be made. In some cases you become an object of curiosity, like some weird species of animal who walks around in a cage of your own devising. In others, you experience hostility, which you can respond to militantly, philosophically, or submissively according to your character. It is not enough to *be* a vegetarian: you have to acquire the ability to justify your choice of diet to the carnivorous majority.

Such psychological pressures on new vegetarians can be considerable, and are too little recognized. The vegetarian Establishment should do more to let new converts know exactly what they are letting themselves in for. It takes time, and not a little determination, to accustom yourself to the fact that you are no longer in the dietary majority. From the moment you give up meat the world becomes a different place. You can no longer eat where you please; doors previously open are now closed to you. Even today a journey away from home can be a major undertaking as far as finding suitable food is concerned, and on top of these practical difficulties are a host of little annoyances you are forced to put up with when your diet doesn't conform.

If you spend much time away from home you may find it helpful to carry a copy of the *International Vegetarian Handbook* with you. Vegetarian and wholefood restaurants may be more numerous than they were a few years ago, but there will always be occasions when you will have to take pot-luck. I shall always remember, in the days when I ate meat, sitting next to a vegetarian at dinner in a Cardiff hotel. There was nothing on the menu that the poor chap could have, and so he asked for some cheese with the main course vegetables. This he duly got — covered with gravy.

If possible, notify your hotel or restaurant in advance of your dietary preferences. It is always worth playing safe, even though these days most places will do their best to accommodate you and it is becoming usual for well-run restaurants to have at least one special vegetarian dish on the menu. If the establishment is clearly not used to dealing with vegetarians, be prepared to ask questions: is there meat in that innocent-seeming quiche? Is the onion soup made with meat stock? Does the spaghetti come with a meat sauce?

The feeling of initial alienation can certainly weigh heavily from time to time; on the other hand, new vegetarians often report feelings of well being, even euphoria. But both extremes are usually short lived, and once the new dietary regime is established there should be no disproportionate highs and lows.

Other changes after abandoning meat may include a decrease in body odour, and an increase in appetite. Eating meat provides more calories than a plant-based diet, so you may be tempted to compensate for this energy loss by eating empty calories. The vegetarian is just as likely to be a junk food addict as the meat-eater, and indeed giving up highly refined convenience products may turn out to be a great deal harder than giving up meat! Snacks are a particular danger: beware of in-between-meal 'treats'. Train yourself to turn instead to fruit, nuts, or even — as a last resort — to the confectionary made from natural ingredients available from health stores.

Whilst a vegetarian diet will not guarantee that you will lose weight, neither is it automatically fattening. Weight gain, whether you are a vegetarian or a carnivore, is a matter of individual metabolism in combination with the amount of food you eat and how much exercise you take.

Protein

The question of protein sufficiency seems to be foremost in people's minds whenever the question of vegetarian nutrition is raised, so much so that it has become something of an obsession with both vegetarian apologists and their opponents, and 'Will I get enough protein?' is often the main worry of the new vegetarian as a result. Who can blame people for worrying when a journalist can write that 'a major hazard in all vegetarian diets which severely restrict animal meats is the lack of sufficient complete proteins . . . The nutritional elements in vegetables are so widely dispersed [whatever that means] that packing all essential amino acids into each day's meal is tough for the most skilled cook.'[1]

It can be stated straight away that there *is* no protein problem for any vegetarian with a minimum of common sense. True, meat is high in protein; but human beings need *protein*, not meat.

The UK Recommended Daily Intake of protein for an average man is 68 grams, which includes a 20 per cent individual variation cushion. A lacto-vegetarian — one that eats milk products — will get 63 grams by eating a pretty spartan menu of a cup of oatmeal, two slices of toast, a peanut butter sandwich, a cup of beans, 2 glasses of milk, and an ounce of cheese. In practice, the intake will be much higher.

Compare this RDI with the recommendation of Carl von Voit, a nineteenth-century German nutritionist: 118 grams of protein per day. In America von Voit's disciple W. O. Atwater recommended 145 grams of protein daily for a labourer and 125 grams for a sedentary worker, on the assumption that hard physical work required a higher intake of protein. We now know that protein needs, on the whole, remain relatively constant whatever job one does — exceptions include recovery from illness or surgery. A lone voice at the turn of the century in favour of a low-protein diet was R. H. Chittenden of Yale, who was convinced that a daily protein intake of 35-50 grams was sufficient. History seems to have proved Chittenden right. Recommended levels have been steadily decreasing as nutritional science becomes more sophisticated. The high-protein myth has been perpetuated in health literature by several well-known writers, including Adelle Davis, who proposed in *Let's Eat Right to Keep Fit* that ignorance of protein was 'the greatest hindrance to good health', and that 'if you wish to maintain your attractiveness, vigour, and youthfulness as long as is humanly possible, it is probably wise to eat considerably more than the [National Research Council] requirements'. [2] Rodger Doyle, in *The Vegetarian Handbook*, points out that views like this have undoubtedly contributed to some of the scepticism about the nutritional sufficiency of vegetarian diets:

> I once asked a group of vegetarians and would-be vegetarians, 'What's the most difficult nutrient to supply in a vegetarian diet?' Almost all of them said, 'Protein.' Their fears are unfounded. If you are on a reasonably well-balanced diet — either lacto-vegetarian or vegan — you need have no fear of getting inadequate protein. Even during the critical periods of growth, pregnancy, and lactation — periods when protein needs are highest — well-planned diets will provide enough. [3]

This is not just special pleading by a vegetarian. Nearly all modern nutrition textbooks back up this view. For instance: 'A vegetarian diet can be made entirely adequate in quality of proteins by the liberal use of legumes and cereal products, and by supplementing vegetable proteins with milk and milk products or with eggs.' [4]

In spite of this, it is still widely believed that meat is a 'first-class' protein, and that giving up meat will necessarily result in having to accept 'second-class' substitutes. Again, this is not the case.

The distinctive feature of proteins is that, as well as carbon, hydrogen, and oxygen, they all contain nitrogen. Whereas carbon, hydrogen, and oxygen are found in carbohydrates and fats, only proteins contain nitrogen. Human beings, as well as all other animals and most plants, cannot use nitrogen directly: plants require it in the form of nitrates in the soil, while humans and animals need it in the form of proteins.

The two main functions of proteins are to promote structural growth and repair worn or damaged tissue, and to maintain supplies of enzymes, hormones, and antibodies. They are made up of amino acids, of which there are two sorts, 'essential' and 'non-essential'. Essential amino acids are those which cannot be synthesized by the body and which must therefore be present in food. These are: methionine, tryptophan, lysine, leucine, isoleucine, phenylalanine, threonine, and valine. Growing children need two more: arginine and histidine.

Non-essential amino acids, on the other hand, are those which the body can manufacture for itself, though they are, in spite of their name, every bit as essential for health as the essential amino acids.

Any protein that contains sufficient quantities of all the eight essential amino acids can be said to be a complete, or 'first-class', protein. It is true that animal proteins — meat, milk, and eggs — meet this requirement and that plant proteins are generally deficient in one or more of the essential amino acids. Egg protein, for example, is almost completely utilized by the body, and is given a Net Protein Utilization (NPU) value of around 94 per cent. But meat and poultry actually have low NPUs — about 30 per cent protein. Milk, on the other hand, has a high NPU (82 per cent). Thus if meat is cut out of the diet, milk, milk products, and eggs would supply you with more than enough protein.

So how can we sum up the plant versus animal protein question? By reminding ourselves that here, as in so many areas of life, it's *quality*, not *quantity*, that counts. As Vic Sussman has pointed out: 'Just because plant foods differ from animal foods in the amounts and patterns of their essential amino acids doesn't mean a vegetarian must eat with a shoehorn to get an adequate amount of protein. An amino acid is an amino acid regardless of its source.'[5]

The point is that the distinction between complete and incomplete (or first- and second-class) proteins is a misleading one, and in any case it should not be made on the basis of individual cases; that is to say, plant proteins in combination can easily supply all the essential amino acids and can therefore be regarded collectively as providing a complete protein source that is in every way comparable to meat.

Eating beans and wheat together at one meal provides a Net Protein Utilization value almost equal to beef, and by combining vegetable proteins in one meal the resulting biological value is equal to, and often greater than, most meats.[6]

Combination, then, is usually seen as the basis of protein sufficiency in a vegetarian diet. For example, several vegetable sources of protein are deficient in methionine, whereas most cereals contain a sufficient amount of this amino acid but are deficient in lysine. Seed and leaf proteins should therefore be eaten together and any animal-derived proteins that are eaten, such as eggs, cheese, or milk, should be mixed with vegetable proteins at the same meal. If vegetable proteins are combined in such ways they cannot be distinguished nutritionally from those of animal origin. As we have already seen, it is the *amino acids* that are important, not the amount of protein *per se*.

To ensure complete and correct utilization of the amino acids it is essential to combine proteins with carbohydrates: taken separately, the utilization of the nitrogen in the amino acids is affected. So eat them together — e.g. bread and cheese, nut roast and potatoes, macaroni and cheese. Thus protein complementation can be reduced to three simple guidelines:

1. Grains × legumes
2. Legumes × seeds
3. Milk, milk products, eggs × all plant proteins.

The idea of protein complementarity, which was advocated by Frances Moore Lappé in her influential book *Diet for a Small Planet*, is very much the received line in vegetarian nutrition. But there is another point of view.

This is based on the fact that protein is actually one of the easiest nutrients to obtain, so much so that the basic dietary requirement of protein is available from a completely random selection of plant foods: 'Through a careless selection of foods, one might develop deficiencies of iron, vitamin A, or vitamin C; but it is almost impossible to develop a protein deficiency on a calorically adequate diet.'[7]

It is thus not necessary to embark on a complex system of food complementing, since plant protein is not only freely available, it is also just as good as animal protein. Some plant protein amino acid patterns — for instance, potatoes — are in fact superior to meat proteins.

The usual method of determining sufficiency of protein intake is a nitrogen balance experiment. If the body's intake of nitrogen through food equals or exceeds overall nitrogen loss, then the body is in nitrogen balance and is getting enough protein. Experiments have shown conclusively that several common plant foods that are not particularly high in protein are nevertheless capable of maintaining nitrogen balance, even when they are the only source of protein in the diet. Corn, wheat, and rice have all been the subjects of such experiments; and potatoes, like rice, have also been shown to maintain nitrogen balance, again when they are the sole source of dietary protein.

The evidence seems impressive. The most forceful campaigner for this new view of protein is Keith Akers, whose conclusion is worth quoting in full:

> Almost all studies of protein value have been performed with rats. Yet obviously the protein requirements of humans are radically different from those of rats. Human milk can support the health and growth of human babies. Human milk, though, with 6% of its calories as protein, *cannot* support the growth of baby rats. Should we assume that if human milk cannot support the growth of baby rats it cannot support human babies either? Yet assumptions about the differences between animal and plant proteins carried over from being a theory about rats to being a theory about humans.
>
> It is time for nutritional theory to grow up. We cannot continue to base our judgements of human protein requirements on the results of experiments on laboratory rats. Let us discard protein complementarity — however valid it might be for protein theory — as a guide to practical human nutrition. [8]

Is protein deficiency therefore impossible for a vegetarian? The answer, from Akers' point of view, seems to be: yes — to all practical purposes. Unless someone is actually starving — i.e. suffering from deficiencies of *all* the vital nutrients, not just protein — there seems little chance of protein malnutrition. In the West, only a diet consisting solely of junk foods could be potentially dangerous for adults. As Akers observes: 'A diet of beer and oatmeal . . . while it would be a very, very bad diet, lacking such essential nutrients as vitamins A and C, would provide the recommended allowance of protein . . . Virtually all vegetables, legumes, grains, nuts, and seeds contain more than enough protein to sustain the growth and maintenance needs of body tissues.' [9]

The moral would seem to be: keep half an eye on food combinations, but do not lose any sleep about protein deficiency if you are following a sensible and varied vegetarian or vegan diet. Most of the basic vegetable foods (but not fruits) are adequate protein sources; dairy products (if you are a lacto-vegetarian), soyabeans, and green leafy vegetables are all good sources; beans and unrefined grains are better sources than most nuts and seeds. The main danger of protein inadequacy is when calories are cut drastically, most usually on a strict slimming diet. Vegetarians who need to slim should seek special advice (two helpful books are noted in the Reading List).

Vitamin B$_{12}$

This is one of the more recently discovered vitamins and is the only one to contain a metal — cobalt. Though only minute quantities are needed by the body (about 3 micrograms a day), vitamin B$_{12}$ is generally held to be of crucial importance: a deficiency can lead to female infertility, nervous disorders, and megaloblastic anaemia. An acute deficiency can result in degeneration of the spinal cord leading to permanent injury or even death. It is thus easy to see why vitamin B$_{12}$, like protein, is one of the 'hot' vegetarian issues. And yet some vegetarians and even vegans insist that B$_{12}$ supplementation is unnecessary:

> There is a widespread belief espoused by popular nutritionists that unless we eat animal products or swallow laboratory fabricated supplements, our bodies are in danger of developing pernicious anaemia due to vitamin B$_{12}$ deficiency.
>
> This is a tremendous hoax which has been created by the wealthy interests of the meat packing houses and processing plants. It is just another lie designed to frighten people into buying animal products.[10]

This is strong stuff and typical of the shrill militancy that often antagonizes those it is meant to persuade. Some might also think it a little irresponsible. So what of the substance of this claim? Can we really live without either animal sources or supplements of B$_{12}$?

The article just quoted from goes on to point out that B$_{12}$ is heat and water soluble and that it is therefore lost when foods are cooked: 'the addition of cooked meat or pasteurized dairy products to our diet will in no way prevent B$_{12}$ deficiency anaemia . . .' How, then, can vegetarians and vegans obtain B$_{12}$?

Vitamin B_{12}, unlike other most essential nutrients, is not manufactured by plants (nor is vitamin D, but the body can synthesize this). It is also unique amongst vitamins in being produced by the activity of micro-organisms. It is then transmitted via animals and animal products to humans. Though it was once thought that no plant source with any significant amount of B_{12} existed it is now known that certain fermented soya foods (e.g. Tempeh) and some sea vegetables (e.g. Kombu) are rich in B_{12}. It is also generally thought that we can synthesize B_{12} by means of a bacteria in the intestinal tract, though beneficial flora can be destroyed by putrefactive organisms originating from meat, cooked foods, and chemical preservatives. It is further thought that eating raw foods, organically grown, in proper combinations and avoiding chemically preserved foods will allow the natural synthesis of B_{12}.

In spite of this, many vegetarians and vegans feel safer taking B_{12} supplements. For lacto-ovo-vegetarians, milk, cheese and eggs provide sufficient B_{12}, though again synthetic supplements will do no harm.

The lack of B_{12} in a 'pure' vegetarian diet is a sore point for many. Whence this flaw in the all-plant diet, held by some to be man's natural diet?

In the first place, as just mentioned, only minute amounts of the vitamin are required. The liver contains several milligrams of B_{12} and is capable of storing it for several years. Secondly, the evidence for the supposedly dire consequences of B_{12} deficiency is actually far from conclusive. Pernicious anaemia, for instance (to which meat-eaters are just as prone as vegetarians), results from an inability to absorb B_{12} itself, whilst megaloblastic anaemia can be caused by a deficiency of folacin, which with B_{12} is needed for DNA synthesis. Many of the examples of B_{12} deficiency cited in the literature also involve other deficiencies, such as folacin and iron; but still lack of B_{12} is assumed to be the sole cause of the problem in these cases. The conclusion of Dr Richard Bargen, an American doctor who surveyed the available evidence in great detail, was that:

> After careful review of all the literature, often quoted as demonstrating 'pure' vegetarians often suffer vitamin B_{12} deficiency because of inadequate dietary intake, not one solitary case was found wherein a vegan, consuming an adequate, purely plant food diet suffered any ill health due to vitamin B_{12} deficiency or any other deficiency. This

finding contradicts the statements made in virtually every textbook of medicine and nutrition I've come across. [11]

Carbohydrates

These are in abundance in most moderate vegetarian diets. The principal sources are most vegetables, grains, fruits, and sugars. The social and cultural correlations to carbohydrate sources are interesting: in the poorer countries of the world predominant carbohydrates differ from those in more affluent countries. In Asia, for example, the main source is rice; in the USA processed sources, often sugar based, predominate. Whilst the amount of cereals, breads, and potatoes has decreased in the typical western diet, the consumption of refined carbohydrates has increased, with resulting nutritional inadequacies.

There is a crucial difference between valuable carbohydrates and those that are 'empty' (apart from their calorific content) and which contribute nothing of nutritional benefit to the diet. Carbohydrates are necessary for normal metabolic functioning and for supplying energy. They include simple sugars (fructose, galactose, and glucose), disaccharides (lactose, maltose, and sucrose), and polysaccharides (cellulose, glycogen, and starch). Refined carbohydrates contain only calories and should therefore be avoided as far as possible: for instance, refined sugar, be it coloured white or brown, is empty of vitamins, minerals, and bulk, but is full of calories. If you need a sweetener use raw cane sugar, blackstrap molasses (which contains calcium, magnesium, iron, and potassium), or honey. Eating refined sugar, by itself or in other foods, causes a rapid rise in blood sugar level, which soon falls again, leaving a craving for more sugar. Unrefined carbohydrates do not have this effect and provide energy in conjunction with nutrients and essential fibre.

Calcium

The provision of calcium — like iron (see below) — can be a problem for strict vegetarians who abstain from milk and dairy products, which are important sources. Careful, though not neurotic, dietary surveillance is thus advisable for such people.

The bulk of calcium in the body (some 99 per cent) is found in the bones and teeth, and in an adult accounts for about 2 per cent of body weight. Calcium is also necessary for muscular responses, blood clotting, and enzyme reaction, amongst other things.

It is important to remember that too much protein intake has the tendency to limit the amount of calcium the body can absorb.

For lacto-vegetarians milk and dairy products will supply ample amounts of calcium: a daily yogurt, 2 oz of hard cheese, an average portion of cottage cheese, and two cups of milk yields about 500-600mg. For vegans, calcium is available in leafy greens such as kale, in soyabeans, sesame seeds, blackstrap molasses, figs, dates, and apricots (see below). Calcium is rendered unusable to the body by oxalic acid, which means that vegetables containing this substance, such as spinach, chard and beet greens, are ruled out as sources.

Iron

Iron is essential for the formation of haemoglobin, which carries oxygen to the tissues. Iron deficiency is a common disorder, but it is not confined to strict vegetarians: many meat-eaters suffer from it. Amongst the reasons are the increased consumption of refined foods that are low in iron, and the decline in use of cast-iron cooking pots and utensils, which actually contributed significant amounts of dietary iron. One American estimate indicates that the available iron in food can be increased by 100-400 per cent when iron cookware is used.

As vitamin C increases the absorption of iron, vegetarians have an advantage over meat-eaters since their diets tend to include more fresh citrus fruits. Iron obtained from animal sources (liver is the richest) is absorbed more efficiently by the body than plant-derived iron, so that though spinach is a good source the iron it contains is not easily assimilated. The main exceptions to this are soyabeans and soyabean products. The iron in eggs is also more readily absorbed than that in plant foods. Tea, and coffee to a lesser extent, inhibits iron absorption. Several studies indicate that the intake of iron from normal vegetarian and vegan diets is adequate, but it is often advised that women, especially during pregnancy, should also take iron supplements.

Deficiency Risks

A typical vegetarian diet, which includes a variety of fresh fruits and vegetables, will supply all the essential vitamins, minerals, and trace elements that adults and children require. The only major exception, as already mentioned, is the case of B_{12} in vegan diets, and here any potential deficiency can be overcome by supplementation.

Iron deficiency is a worry for some vegetarians, especially expectant mothers. In theory, vegetarians are at risk in this respect because, as we have seen, iron from plant sources is not so easily absorbed as that from meat. On the other hand, beans, dried fruit, and some vegetables are high in iron, and eggs are a valuable source if your diet allows them. Absorption of iron is increased by vitamin C, so your diet should contain plenty of fresh citrus fruits and vegetables rich in vitamin C (see below). One British expert, Dr F. R. Ellis, showed that vegans actually have fewer iron deficiency symptoms than people who follow an omnivorous diet. If you are in any doubt about your iron intake, or suspect you may be anaemic, consult your doctor or nutritionist immediately.

Zinc deficiency is a relatively recent concern. The symptoms are the slow healing of wounds and a loss of ability to taste and smell. Plant sources of zinc are inferior to meat, which has caused some nutritionists to believe that vegetarians may be at risk in this respect. Marginal zinc deficiency is not a problem for healthy adults, but again, if you are worried you should seek advice.

Calcium deficiency can be a worry for new vegans, who do not of course take milk or dairy products in their diet. Calcium is available in large amounts in whole sesame seeds, broccoli, and kale, and in fact adult vegans have little difficulty in exceeding the daily calcium allowance advocated by the World Health Organization (400-500 milligrams daily). If you are unsure whether your daily allowance is reaching this level you can drink calcium-fortified soya milk — either commercially prepared or homemade soya milk with added calcium. Homemade bread can also be fortified with added calcium carbonate (available from chemists).

Checklist Of Selected Sources

Protein Sources
Barley, brown rice, buckwheat, oats, wheat, wheat germ, millet, beans (broad, mung, butter [lima], kidney, soya), chickpeas, lentils, peas,

pumpkin seeds, sesame seeds, sunflower seeds, almonds, brazil nuts, coconuts, peanuts, walnuts, milk, dairy products, eggs.

Calcium Sources
Parmesan cheese, whole sesame seeds, skim milk, plain yogurt, carrageenan, Edam cheese, Cheddar cheese, cottage cheese, blackstrap molasses, apricots, dates, broccoli stalks, soyabeans, dried figs, sour cream, turnips, butter (lima) beans, kidney beans, shelled almonds, cabbage, artichokes, fortified soya milk, fortified brewer's yeast, tahini (sesame paste or butter), sunflower seeds, kale.

Carbohydrate Sources
Wholegrain cereals, vegetables, fruit.

Iron Sources
Prune juice, butter (lima) beans, soyabeans, kidney beans, lentils, spinach, split peas, pumpkin seeds, Swiss chard, raisins, dates, watermelon, sunflower seeds, dried apricots, kale, tomato juice, wholewheat bread, wholegrain cereals, strawberries, brewer's yeast, oatmeal, artichokes, blackberries, broccoli, lettuce, brown rice, leafy greens, molasses.

Phosphorus Sources
Eggs, wheat germ, wholegrains, oatmeal, brewer's yeast, cheese, nuts, dried beans.

Sodium Sources
Milk, eggs, seaweed, sea salt.

Potassium Sources
Yeast, potatoes, molasses, bran, bananas, oranges, many fruits and vegetables.

Magnesium Sources
Green vegetables, seaweed, soya flour, nuts, tofu, molasses, wholegrains, sesame seeds.

Sulphur Sources
Cheese, peanuts, wheat germ, kidney beans, lentils.

Zinc Sources
Eggs, milk, cheese, seaweed, wholegrains, legumes, pumpkin seeds.

Chromium Sources
Wholegrains, brewer's yeast, fruits, vegetables.

Cobalt Sources
Milk, seaweed.

Copper Sources
Nuts, wholegrains, green leafy vegetables, brewer's yeast, dried legumes.

Manganese Sources
Wheat bran, most vegetables, fruit, wholegrains, peanut butter.

Molybdenum Sources
Wholegrain cereals, brewer's yeast.

Selenium Sources
Seaweed, milk, wheat, brewer's yeast.

Iodine Source
Kelp.

VITAMIN SOURCES

Vitamin A
Egg yolks, butter, margarine (polyunsaturated), carrots, sweet potatoes, kale, tomatoes, spinach, apricots, pumpkins.

B complex
  B_1 *(Thiamine)*: brewer's yeast, wheat germ, peas, soyabeans, wholegrain cereals, oranges [n.b. B_1 is destroyed by heat].

  B_2 *(Riboflavin)*: brewer's yeast, milk, wholegrains, almonds, Brazil nuts, leafy greens, cheese, eggs.

  B_3 *(Niacin)*: brewer's yeast, peanut butter, wholemeal bread, wholegrain cereals.

  B_6 *(Pyridoxine)*: egg yolks, brewer's yeast, bananas, wholegrains, vegetables.

Folic acid: widely available in plants, lettuce, legumes, spinach, mushrooms, nuts, wholegrains, oranges, bananas.

Pantothenic acid: egg yolks, peas, butter (lima) beans, broccoli, wheat bran, brewer's yeast.

Biotin: egg yolks, mung bean sprouts, milk, soyabeans (cooked), some fruits, vegetables, and nuts.

B_{12}: plain yogurt, cottage cheese, eggs, skim milk, whole milk, cheese (various), spirulina, fortified brewer's yeast, fortified soya milk, some varieties of seaweed.

Vitamin C: raw fruits and vegetables, citrus fruits, strawberries, green pepper, cauliflower, tomatoes, potatoes, broccoli.

To sum up: the key to sound vegetarian nutrition is to take advantage of the variety of plant foods that is now available. Don't restrict yourself to a narrow diet — a particular temptation for new vegetarians. Dropping meat from your diet is only the first step; you should explore the many possibilities of your new diet.

Remember that it is not true that a vegetarian diet is complex and difficult to maintain in comparison with one based on meat; it does not involve constant vigilance or demanding study, simply a basic awareness of nutritional facts and common sense. Equip yourself with a good selection of vegetarian cookbooks (see Reading List).

Dark green leafy vegetables (e.g. kale, broccoli, spinach, watercress, parsley, collards, turnip greens) are particularly nutritious. Plant foods in general provide all the major nutrients essential for an active and creative life, as well as the minor nutrients such as phosphorus, copper, chromium, selenium, and molybdenum. No vegetarian diet that contains a reasonable variety of fresh vegetables, wholegrains, nuts, and seeds should be nutritionally deficient in any way.

Are Humans Natural Carnivores?
There is no irrefutable evidence that humans are either naturally carnivorous or naturally vegetarian, though there are several factors that seem to suggest a closer physiological relationship with non-carnivorous species.

Animal carnivores — the cat family, wolves, bears, foxes, dogs, etc — have canine teeth and jaw structures that make them highly efficient at biting and tearing flesh food, but which are of little use for grinding or chewing. On the other hand, herbivores — for instance, horses, goats, cows, and deer — are fitted with teeth and jaw structures that allow them to grind and chew tough vegetation.

Humans *do* have canine teeth, but they are virtually vestigial and ineffectual in comparison with real carnivores. Overall, our dental structure allies us more with herbivorous animals than with the flesh-eaters. Carnivores have short bowels, for rapid expulsion of putrefactive bacteria inherent in flesh foods; herbivores, like humans, have long bowels, for dealing with fermentative bacteria in plant foods. Carnivores do not sweat through the skin: their body heat is controlled by rapid breathing and extrusion of the tongue. Herbivores have sweat pores for heat control and elimination of impurities. Carnivores secrete large quantities of hydrochloric acid to dissolve bones; herbivores do not. Carnivores lap water, like a cat; herbivores take in liquids by suction.

So what should we conclude? Are we naturally carnivorous? No, not in a strict sense, but we can eat meat. Are we naturally omnivorous? We have few physiological resemblances to animal omnivores (e.g. bears), but we can eat a wide range of plant and animal foods. Are we then naturally frugivorous or herbivorous? Again, yes and no.

What about our nearest animal relatives, the apes? Humans and African apes are very close physiologically speaking, sharing virtually similar DNA structure and many other common features. On this basis it was long held that because our nearest animal relatives didn't eat meat, our natural diet must be a vegetarian one. However, modern field studies — notably by Jane Goodall in Tanzania — have shown that wild chimpanzees do in fact occasionally kill and eat flesh (e.g. monkeys, small baboons, even on occasion human babies). This craving for flesh seemed to go in phases, triggered off by a chance encounter with easy prey; but these periods were infrequent, and observations elsewhere have not provided correlative evidence for this pattern of behaviour. Gorillas, however, are completely vegetarian in the wild, eating only plants and fruit.

Some anthropologists view Man as a natural killer, on the theory that primitive humans had to kill and eat meat or perish. An opposing view is that early hominids (like chimpanzees) lived principally on plant foods and only ate meat in the form of abandoned carcasses. The fact is, we simply do not know the truth; but a broad view of the available evidence suggests that Man is Nature's greatest opportunist. He can be a hunter, a grubber of roots, a gatherer, a forager, a farmer — anything at all, in fact, that will provide him with the nutrients he needs to stay alive. This adaptability and ingenuity indeed is why the species has survived and prospered: it has never been limited to a specific area or environment by a specialized, restricted diet: it can live almost anywhere. This does not diminish the claims of vegetarianism, which, objectively speaking, is only one of a number of possible human diets. If man is a natural killer he is also a natural philosopher, moralist, mystic, and artist. With his instincts for cruelty and aggression there exists an impulse towards compassion and creativity. Which should we strive to uncover and develop? For vegetarians, the choice is clear.

All this points to the conclusion that humans are not naturally carnivores, frugivores, herbivores, or omnivores, but are uniquely adaptable to a wide range of diets, allowing considerable scope for individual variation and preferences. We can eat meat, but there is nothing, in physiological and nutritional terms, that compels us to do so. The *only* practical consideration is adequate nourishment. Both meat-eating and vegetarianism, then, are 'natural' to us. But which is best for us?

Meat and Modern Disease

It is one of the great ironies of the twentieth century that as medical science has virtually eradicated or at least controlled many of the killer diseases of the past others have risen up in their place. In developed countries, the threat of infectious diseases has largely been replaced by that of degenerative diseases — the so-called diseases of civilization, such as cancer, heart disease, and obesity. Apart from any other considerations, the economic cost of treating degenerative diseases is astronomical, and increasing every year.

The cumulative evidence of intensive research over the last few decades is that diet is the single most important factor in the proliferation of these diseases in the West. (For example, in 1983 the NACNE Report in the UK concluded that poor diet was a major factor in contemporary disease patterns.) The diet in question has two main constituents: refined (or convenience, or processed, or just plain junk) foods, and meat.

Meat is a problem in three ways: it contains too much fat, too much protein, and no fibre. A diet based on meat and refined foods must result in high fat and high protein intake, both of which are undesirable. When one adds the lack of dietary fibre, which we now know to be essential, we have — quite literally — a recipe for disaster. Let's look at these three items in turn.

The Fat Problem

The consumption of animal fats has been implicated in the growing incidence of heart disease and some forms of cancer, as well as other things. One American nutritionist has calculated that some 50 per cent of cancers in the USA could be attributed to a meat-based diet that is also high in processed foods. The same researcher also maintained that a person who eats two 12-ounce charcoal-broiled steaks a week gets more tar than from smoking two packets of cigarettes a day for the same period. (In the UK, the connections between meat-eating and cancer are being investigated by Sir Richard Doll, the Oxford professor of medicine who helped establish the smoking-lung cancer link.)

It is terrifyingly easy for us to take on more fat than is good for us. Bacon contains 80 per cent fat (as a percentage of calories), 18 per cent protein, and only 2 per cent carbohydrates. Ground beef contains 40 per cent fat, 51 per cent protein, and no carbohydrates. The great British favourite, chips (French fries), contain 80 times more fat than a potato, whilst crisps, another widely consumed item, contain 120 times more fat than a potato. Even lean meat derives 20-30 per cent of its calories from fat; for other meats, the figure is much higher. Over 50 per cent of the fat in the typical American diet derives from animal foods: looking at it another way, the average American is getting over 40 per cent of his calories from fat, and what is true of America is fast becoming true for a growing proportion of other populations in developed countries.

There are three types of fat to be aware of: (1) *saturated fats*, derived mainly from animal sources (lard, butter, muscle meats, etc); (2) *unsaturated fats*, deriving mainly from vegetable and seed oils; and (3) *hydrogenated fats*, which are polyunsaturated fats that have been converted to solids or semi-solids by the addition of hydrogen (polyunsaturated fats are liquid at room temperature: hydrogenated fats are found in a number of processed foods). For vegetarians, polyunsaturated fats are specified (e.g. vegetable oil for cooking, polyunsaturated margarine, etc).

But it is not just meat-eaters who are prone to excessive fat intake; indeed lacto-vegetarians are particularly vulnerable in this respect since they tend to compensate for not eating meat with a surfeit of fatty foods. Whilst cheese is a rich source of protein many varieties are high in fat; and many moderate vegetarians consume large quantities of eggs, butter, milk, and cream without giving a thought either to the possible health dangers or to the ethical consequences. (The egg industry is one of the most ruthless intensive forms of modern factory farming; milk production also involves cruelty, for a cow needs to be made pregnant periodically in order to prevent her milk from drying up. Each calf is taken away from the mother to be slaughtered or raised for veal, and this separation undoubtedly causes anguish to both mother and calf.)

Perhaps because of fears over possible protein deficiency, many vegetarians have been eating diets that are rich in animal fat, which in some cases may have cancelled out the nutritional benefits they have gained from giving up meat. This situation led one vegetarian to reflect how easy it was to get into a rut:

> Not so long ago I realized that I was making such a big point of obtaining 'vegetarian' cheese (i.e. without animal rennet) that I was quite overlooking the fact that my dependence on dairy products was actually growing! . . . It suddenly came home to me one day that this increased consumption of dairy products was probably harming more animals than my fussing about rennet helped; so I made an effort to cut down my overall consumption of dairy products as much as possible by introducing tofu and soya milk into my diet and experimenting more with vegan recipes. [12]

High Protein and Lack of Fibre

Many meat-eaters are actually getting more protein than they need, in some cases twice as much. High intake of protein increases excretion of calcium, which results in a loss of bone mass (osteoporosis) and increased susceptibility to fractures, puts increased strain on the liver and kidneys, and shortens life expectancy. In an American study of 1000 people it was shown that bone calcium was at dangerously low levels in the meat-eaters compared with the vegetarians. (Vegetarians in general have significantly greater bone densities than omnivores.)

Excessive protein intake has also been linked with obesity, diabetes, and cancer of the colon, and some researchers have suggested that the key factor in atherosclerosis may be high levels of protein rather than cholesterol or saturated fats. High protein intake can also result in vitamin losses. As one expert has noted: 'Contrary to conventional "wisdom", it is the meat-based — not the vegetarian-based — diet that presents the greater difficulties in obtaining adequate nutrition, that requires the more complex "computations" and careful "combinations".'[13]

Whilst meat is capable of providing too much protein in the diet, it can never provide enough fibre, which is abundantly available with plant foods. Low-fibre foods predominate in the modern refined diet — meat (accounting for some 20 per cent of the diet), refined cereals (18 per cent), refined fats (18 per cent), sugar (17 per cent), milk (12 per cent), eggs, and alcohol (2 per cent each). High-fibre foods typically only account for about 11 per cent of the diet. The British scientist Dr Denis Burkitt and many others have linked bowel cancer, appendicitis, and diverticulosis with a low fibre diet that is also high in refined foods. Fibre has become a fashionable health subject in recent years, but there is no doubt that the vogue rests on solid factual foundations. Fibre facilitates a speedy evacuation of bodily wastes, thus helping to keep the colon free of accumulated and potentially harmful debris. Transit time through the gastro-intestinal tract is on average 30 hours on an unrefined diet, compared with 77 hours on a refined diet. Amongst the things a swift transit time helps guard against is the production of bile acids in the gastro-intestinal tract, which is important because there is a correlation between cancer of the colon and increased production of bile acids. Dr Michael J. Hill, writing in *The Lancet,* pointed out in this connection that: 'People living in the areas with a high recorded incidence of carcinoma of the colon tend to live on diets containing large amounts of fat and animal protein; whereas those who live in areas with a low incidence live on largely vegetarian diets with little fat or animal matter.'[14]

Certain types of fibre — e.g. in oats and legumes — also help to lower serum cholesterol, which decreases the likelihood of coronary heart disease. Individuals with a low intake of roughage are accustomed to a constant degree of constipation, which increases the chances of developing haemorrhoids and bowel disorders. On average, a typical vegetarian diet will yield from two to three times more roughage than a meat-based diet.

Heart Disease

Heart disease is one of the major killers of our time. Though there are other factors involved, it is now generally recognized that there is a correlation between a meat-based diet and atherosclerosis — a thickening of the arteries that can cause heart attacks, strokes, and other coronary problems.

However, it is still not completely clear what specifically causes atherosclerosis. Various candidates have been put forward: cholesterol, sugar, protein, vitamin B_6 deficiency, smoking, saturated fat, or a combination of several factors. But one thing is clear: meat consumption is a critical variable, whilst a vegetarian diet is one that will substantially reduce or prevent atherosclerosis. If the cause is cholesterol, then a diet rich in plant foods, which contain no cholesterol, is to be recommended; if saturated fats are isolated as the single cause of atherosclerosis, the same is true, for plant foods are low in these. If a preventative diet is to be low in protein and sugar, then again a vegetarian diet is the answer; if high levels of vitamin B_6 are called for, this too favours the adoption of a vegetarian diet.

There are two well-known examples of how a drastic reduction in the consumption of animal fats has an effect on the pattern of health and disease of a specific population. During the Second World War, when Norway was occupied by the Nazis, meat, whole milk, cheese, cream and eggs were scarce and the Norwegians were obliged to eat more fish, cereals, potatoes, vegetables, and skim milk. Because of this change in staple dietary items they ate fewer calories, less fat, less sugar, and less cholesterol, and their consumption of dietary fibre increased. The result was that, during the war, deaths from heart and cardiovascular disease decreased by 21 per cent; to emphasize the point, after the war — when Norway's diet resumed its prewar staples — the former mortality rate from circulatory diseases returned.

The Norwegian experience had in fact been paralleled in Denmark during the First World War twenty years or so earlier. The Allied blockade of the country brought acute food shortages and the Danish government sought the advice of Dr Mikkel Hindhede of the

Laboratory for Nutrition Research in Copenhagen. In the *Journal of the American Medical Association* in 1920 Dr Hindhede described the situation faced by the Danes: 'Our principal foods were bran bread,barley porridge, potatoes, greens, milk and some butter . . . the people of the cities and towns got little or no pork. Beef was so costly that only the rich could afford to buy it in sufficient amount. It is evident, therefore, that most of the population was living on a milk and vegetable diet.' Dr Hindhede's main recommendation was to slaughter the livestock and use the grain that was normally fed to animals as human food. He also had the bread enriched with bran and barley meal, giving the Danes the benefit of a high-fibre food product. 'It was,' said Hindhede, 'a low-protein experiment on a large scale, about three million subjects being available.'

From the period October 1917 to October 1918, at the height of the food restrictions, the overall mortality rate from disease fell to 10.4 deaths per thousand, the lowest on record and representing a drop of 34 per cent on the preceding eighteen years. Of course the Danes also consumed less tobacco and alcohol during this period; but while these were certainly contributory factors, Hindhede was convinced that 'overnutrition, the result of palatable meat dishes, is one of the most common causes of disease.'

The same moràl has emerged from several studies of Seventh-day Adventists in America. The Adventists discourage meat-eating and forbid smoking, thus making them a particularly interesting subject of study for health scientists. One of several reports on the Adventists shows that total vegetarian Adventist men have only 12 per cent of expected coronary heart disease mortality.[15] John Scharffenberg comments:

> This is one of the most revealing studies of the past decade. It points out that not only can heart disease mortality be reduced but that life expectancy can be increased. It also establishes beyond reasonable doubt that saturated fat, and specifically meat, is a factor in heart disease mortality.[16]

Cancer

Several factors are now seen to associate meat with a potential for inducing cancer. They include: the presence in meat of chemical carcinogens; transmission of cancer viruses; lack of fibre; high fat intake; high prolactin levels.

A 2-pound charcoal-broiled steak contains as much benzopyrene, which is known to cause stomach tumours and leukaemia in rats, as the smoke from 600 cigarettes. When meat fat is heated a known carcinogen, methylcholanthrene, is formed: even small levels of this can increase cancer susceptibility. The nitrites added to some meat (e.g. pork products) to enhance appearance can produce carcinogenic agents called nitrosamines when combined with secondary and tertiary amines, which are found naturally in a wide range of foods.

Cancer viruses in animal tumours can be transmitted from species to species: for instance, in 1974 it was demonstrated that chimpanzees fed from birth with milk from cows that had leukaemia died of leukaemia in the first year of life. Clearly, no experiments have been done on humans, but there seems no scientific reason why the human species should be an exception in this regard.

Experiments carried out at the National Cancer Centre Research Institute of Japan has linked early menarche (onset of menstruation) with a greater risk of breast cancer. Rapid maturation can be induced in animals on high-protein diets, again implicating meat as a key factor. Vegetarians, on the other hand, mature more slowly. The high fat content of a meat diet has also been linked with breast cancer. Where consumption of animal fat and animal protein is high (for instance, the USA, Great Britain, Canada, Australia, New Zealand), breast cancer mortality rates increase. The reverse is true where less animal fat, especially beef, is consumed (e.g. the Far East). Japanese women have one of the lowest breast cancer rates in the world, but Japanese women living in America and eating a high-fat, high-protein, highly refined American diet are four times more likely to develop breast cancer than they are in their own country.

A pioneer investigator of the diet-cancer link was Dr Max Gerson in the 1920s and 1930s. His 'anticancer' diet prohibited meat, fish, eggs, butter, fat- and protein-rich foods, tobacco, and alcohol. Since Gerson's time the correlations have become indisputable. One such involves high prolactin levels. Prolactin is a hormone that promotes milk formation and lactation in women and high levels of it have been shown to produce mammary tumour growth in laboratory animals. Keith Akers describes one experiment relating to prolactin:

Four volunteers were put on a control diet and then switched to a vegetarian diet. The vegetarian diet had 33% of calories as fat, as opposed to 40% on the control diet. This might seem like a small difference, but the results were highly significant. Prolactin release began to decline an hour earlier on the vegetarian diet, and was only half of what it was on the control diet at 5 a.m. . . . Peak levels of prolactin secretion occurred at about 4 or 5 in the morning.[15]

Once again, the Seventh-day Adventists provide suggestive evidence. A study published in the American journal *Cancer Research* calculated that the Adventists' rates of nutrition-related cancer (including cancer of the colon, rectum, and intestine) were 50 to 70 per cent lower than for the general population. The study concluded that on statistical evidence, 'the lacto-ovo-vegetarian diet may protect against colon cancer.'[16]

A decade ago, when vegetarians were dismissed as cranks, the person who gave up eating meat was usually characterized as a pale, sickly creature. Now the health benefits of vegetarianism are widely known, and, conversely, the possible detrimental effects of meat-eating realized, the image is very different. It is now known that vegetarians are, on the whole, healthier than the average meat-eater; they appear to have more energy, tend not to have weight problems, and retain a youthful appearance for longer. As we have seen in this chapter, a high meat diet, has been linked with several degenerative diseases, for instance breast cancer, and research has shown that vegetarians are less likely to suffer from high blood pressure and heart attacks.

As well as reducing the risk of breast cancer, a vegetarian diet is good for women in other ways: premenstrual symptoms appear to be eased, and are often eradicated, and on the whole vegetarian women do not suffer from cellulite deposits — the hard fat that accumulates on the thighs and upper arms. It is almost impossible to overeat on a vegetarian diet, which makes for a slimmer figure now and less chance of obesity in later life.

For millions of people in the world, of course, there is no dietary choice. While we in the developed West can opt for a change of diet to suit our convictions, this privilege is denied to countless numbers in the Third World. We have a duty to take care of our own health, and that of our children; but we also have a duty to those for whom every day brings the agonizing pangs of death by starvation a little closer. We have a further duty: to the Earth itself and to our immediate environment. It is in relation to these issues that the vegetarian commitment becomes part of a global context.

4.

COUNTING THE COST

THE sheer scale of modern meat production results in immense human and ecological problems. Livestock agriculture depletes natural resources at such a rate that it simply would not be possible to sustain meat consumption globally on the American scale. It is even doubtful whether there are sufficient resources to sustain *current* levels of meat consumption for more than a generation or two.

Animals are economically and ecologically expensive food sources, and the continuing emphasis on meat as a staple commodity is in fact a contributory factor in world hunger. Cattle, in the words of Frances Moore Lappé, are 'protein factories in reverse'. She points out that it takes approximately 8 units of plant protein to yield 1 unit of animal protein: the remaining 7 units are needed by the animal for its own biological processes.

Put another way, livestock animals on average consume 20 pounds of plant protein for every pound of meat they yield; which clearly shows that it is plant proteins, not animal, that have the real potential for alleviating the world's food problems. A plant creates its protein from water, carbon dioxide, and nitrogen; animals have to eat plants, or other animals, to get their protein. A cow can certainly convert plant foods into protein for human consumption, but at huge cost, both in financial and human terms. These are not new ideas: they have long been recognized and the gross inefficiency of meat production articulated many times over the last decade or so. The link between agricultural inefficiency and global food shortages was pointed out by Senator Hubert Humphrey in 1974, in a speech at the Rennselaer Conference on World Hunger at the United Nations: 'A decision by Americans to eat one less hamburger each week would make some 10 million tons of grain available for food assistance to the starving people of the world.' A year later, in 1975, the English author, Jon Wynne-Tyson wrote: 'We read in our newspapers about the starving and under-fed millions, and all the time we are feeding to meat-producing animals the very crops that could more than eradicate world food shortage; also, we are importing from starving nations large quantities of grain and other foods that are then fed to our animals instead of to the populations who produced them.'[1] But little has changed. Well over 350 million tons of the world's grain harvest is fed to animals every year while some 350 million of the world's children are suffering from malnutrition. Meat is still reared and consumed in vast quantities; the hopeless millions still starve.

Every six seconds someone in the world starves to death — that is, between 10,000 and 14,000 people a day, or three and a half million a year. The American experience again points up the iniquities of a national diet based on meat. Though the statistics are American, the moral is the same for the rest of the developed world. In America, each person is fed by 5 acres of land and the average American consumes 300 pounds of meat per year. This means that some 45 per cent of American arable land is given over to graze livestock, whilst only 17 per cent is used for crops: 'During the final four months of a steer's life, through overfeeding he gains 600 to 800 pounds. During this time he consumes over a ton of feed. Multiply that by the millions of steers all munching away at once, and you've got a situation in which livestock consume 97 per cent of the nation's legumes, 90 per cent of its grain, and 80 per cent of its fish.'[2]

There are other undesirable spin-offs from meat production on a large scale besides the scandalous squandering of land and crop resources. The intensive rearing of animals for meat requires immense amounts of water — for the irrigation of crops to feed livestock, drinking water for the animals, and the water used in meat production. In total, to sustain a meat diet requires eight times more water than it would to support a plant-based diet.

At the same time that meat production *uses* water on a massive scale it also *pollutes* water. The waste matter produced by slaughterhouses — fat, grease, offal, faecal matter, carcases, etc — can create local pollution; but the main problem concerns livestock waste, which is a widespread cause of water pollution. (One might think that it would be logical to use such waste as fertilizer; but in practice it is often cheaper to use chemical fertilizers.) For example, in America many of the areas with water pollution problems are located near areas of intensive livestock rearing (Oklahoma, Kansas, Illinois, the Ohio Valley, the Texas Panhandle).

Deforestation is another problem associated with a high demand for meat because of the conversion of forest to grazing land for livestock. In Latin America one of the prime factors in the terrible acceleration of deforestation is the demand for grazing land for cattle. Between 1950 and 1975 the area of man-established pasture in Central America more than doubled, mostly as a result of clearing tropical forests: 'The major causes of deforestation . . . in the world are inextricably linked to the production of animal foods, especially meat, and the grazing land requirements for cattle. Present trends indicate that the world will experience a crisis in the need for forest products in another generation or two.'[3]

Soil erosion is yet another concomitant of an agricultural economy based on livestock. Throughout history, overgrazing has had serious environmental consequences; this is still a problem, even in developed countries. According to John Block, President Reagan's Secretary of Agriculture, the USA is facing a soil erosion crisis, with 60 per cent of its rangelands being overgrazed. Millions of acres of land are lost each year, both in America and elsewhere, as a result of soil erosion, much of which is attributable to livestock agriculture. It has been calculated that a vegetarian economy would eliminate as much as 90 per cent of this erosion.

Cattle are inefficient food sources on a small scale as well as a large scale, as one jaundiced self-sufficient homesteader came to realize:

> It takes maybe 1½ acres of land to feed an adult on grains and vegetables, but you'll probably have to set aside about 20 acres to feed and graze a cow . . . Even the cost of refrigeration is something we don't want to contend with. As far as I'm concerned, their biggest use lies in their ability to replace a tractor and to give manure and milk.[4]

The meat industry is built on topsy-turvy economic principles. Massive wastage is taken for granted. One estimate puts losses due to disease in British pigs at 137 million pounds a year, 33 million to 'unplanned deaths', 94 million to 'lost production potential', and 10 million to vet and drugs bills. These losses average nearly £10 per pig.

Or take beef cattle. 1200lb of protein a year is required to produce 75lb of meat protein, and this is for an intensively reared beast:

> A grazing steer will produce only 5lb of protein per acre of land and is hopelessly inefficient unless the land is unsuited to any other use. If however you put the steers in a barn, and feed them on barley grown on that same acre of land you can produce 50lb of protein. Grow wheat instead and forget about the steer altogether, and you get 185lb of protein from your acre of land. Switch to growing soya and you could increase the acreage yield to 560lb of protein — ten times the best yield that factory farming can produce.[5]

Factory Farming

Meat in the latter half of the twentieth century is far removed from the fabled 'roast beef of Old England' beloved of our ancestors. It is now a complete 'product'. By the time it reaches the table it has been through a bewildering variety of processes to make it conform to marketing requirements, which spuriously reflect 'what the customer wants'. The long-term effects of such processes are unknown; but already the signs are that they are having undesirable consequences.

The idea of animals being reared for the table in gentle pastoral surroundings is a myth as far as the modern meat industry is concerned. Animal welfare and the profit motive are incompatible. Impersonal, not to say ruthless, corporate logic requires a systematized production line. There is no room for sentimentality, or even simple compassion, down on the factory farm. Let's pause for a moment and remind ourselves what the intensive rearing of animals involves.

Even today, with the proliferation of free range eggs, most of our eggs come from hens that spend miserable lives imprisoned in cages that allow them no room to move. Their natural behaviour patterns are completely destroyed, and after about fifteen months they are thrown out to be slaughtered, often featherless, blind, and lame from their imprisonment. The battery system produces birds that are never allowed to run, scratch the ground, or make a dustbath as they would in a natural environment. They never spread their wings; they never relate to other members of their own species; they can never fulfil their maternal instincts, which are highly developed in hens. The average wing span of a chicken is 32 inches, but they are generally allowed only 4 inches of cage width per bird in battery houses. In order to stimulate egg production, the light intensity in a battery house is maintained for anything up to 18 hours a day. Because of boredom, pecking and even cannibalism is common, which leads to de-beaking of the birds. Hens kept in these conditions produce eggs that often differ in nutritional quality from free range eggs.

Once again, wastage is an accepted fact of life. It is not unusual for a battery egg operation to lose between 10 and 15 per cent of its hens a year, mostly from problems related to the overcrowded and unnatural conditions: 'According to the manager of a 50,000 bird egg ranch [in California] five to ten of his hens succumb daily to confinement stress. (That's between two and four thousand per year.) "Those birds," he says, "don't die of any disease. They just can't take the stress of crowded living."' [6]

Peter Singer has pointed out that 'Of all the animals commonly eaten in the Western world, the pig is without doubt the most intelligent . . . When George Orwell put the pigs in charge of Animal Farm his choice was defensible on scientific as well as literary grounds.' As a consequence of its intelligence a pig is particularly sensitive to its environment and social setting. When they are intensively reared boredom is a very real problem. In confined conditions pigs start to bite each other's tails (the common remedy for which is tail-docking), and they suffer from acute stress, as mentioned earlier (see p. 34). Sows spend their pregnancies in what are called dry-sow stalls. They are forced to lie on concrete floors, slatted at the rear to allow dung and urine to fall through. The slats cause soreness to the back feet of the sow. Because of the constrictions of the stalls lameness and spinal troubles are common. When they are ready to farrow the sows are moved to farrowing pens, which are similarly constricted. Seven days after farrowing the litters are taken away from the sows, who will be stocked again and put back into the dry-sow stalls. As for the piglets, when they are two to three weeks old they are put into battery cages, three tiers high, where they remain until they reach about 100lb liveweight. They are then fattened in pens.

Back in 1965 the Brambell Report recommended a mandatory safeguard for pigs: 'Pregnant sows should not be kept without daily

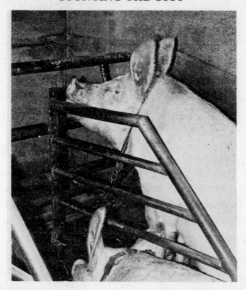

The intensive rearing of pigs. Back in 1965 the Brambell Report recommended that 'pregnant sows should not be kept without daily exercise in quarters which do not permit them to turn round and, in any case, should not be tethered indoors.' *(Photographs: Compassion in World Farming)*

exercise in quarters which do not permit them to turn around and, in any case, should not be tethered indoors.' The practice of intensive close confining of pigs still goes on. One little regarded aspect of the intensive process is the consequences of fire on factory farms. Statistics are hard to come by, but in 1979 Compassion in World Farming quoted a Fire Research Memorandum that estimated that in a single year 200,000 head of livestock were burnt to death while trapped in their cages or stalls.

The same organization provided the following summary of factory farm animals. They

★ compete directly with man for food, consuming oilseed proteins needed in countries where they are grown, in the fight against malnutrition;

★ create the need for continuous corn growing, which in turn calls for more chemical fertilizers, weed-killers and pesticides, to the detriment of the wildlife of the countryside;

★ waste primary food (only 10 per cent efficiency);

★ cause air- and water-pollution;

★ degrade the sensibilities of all who work with them, and

★ threaten health because of the drug residues and pathogens which they pass on in their products and meat. [7]

The 1965 Brambell Report, mentioned earlier, is a seminal document in the modern literature of animal welfare and is still of great interest to all vegetarians. The committee was set up under F. W. Rogers Brambell, a distinguished zoologist, and included an appendix by W. H. Thorpe, director of the Department of Animal Behaviour at Cambridge. (It is interesting to note that the first Professorship of Animal Welfare is being established at Cambridge, as a result of a recognition of the need to promote studies into animal health, the ethical considerations arising from the role of animals in society, and the codes of practice in animal production. In 1985 the Clinical Veterinary Medicine Syndicate at Cambridge stressed the need for further research into the behavioural and physiological bases of animal stress, aggression, and fear — research that relates directly to the exploitative methods of intensive farming.) The Brambell

Report remains essential reading for anyone interested in animal rights and the barbarities of factory farming. In his appendix Thorpe stressed the effects of intensive rearing on animals either used to or conditioned to respond to the freedom of movement and social integration of their natural environments:

> All the domestic animals which man farms are species which, in the wild, show a fairly highly organized social life either in flock, family, clan or herd. This means that their behavioural organization is also potentially on a high level, far higher than the ordinary man imagines. Even though a cow in a stall or a pig in a sty may appear stupid enough, this impression may be quite erroneous simply because we have never even begun to comprehend the social organization of the wild ancestor which in turn, despite the effects of domestication, still undoubtedly determines the sensory abilities and level of feeling and perception of the animal.

What Goes Into Modern Meat

In the pursuit of profit, the meat industry relies heavily on chemical additives of various kinds to 'improve' its products — additives for preservation, colouring, texturing, promoting growth, tranquillizing, and keeping unprofitable illnesses at bay.

Cattle do not roam soft rolling hillsides, contentedly chewing the cud before being humanely dispatched, as some meat-eaters still fondly believe, or try to believe. From birth they are given antibiotics, tranquillizers, and hormones; after slaughtering their carcases are injected with more chemical agents: colourings to make decomposing flesh look 'appetizing' and 'fresh'; sodium nitrite and sodium nitrate to arrest the rate of putrefaction ('Under certain conditions, nitrites combine with amines found in meats and other foods, such as wine and beer, to form nitrosamines, called by the F.D.A. [Food and Drugs Administration] "one of the most formidable and versatile groups of carcinogens yet discovered"'[8]).

The greatest hygiene risks occur during slaughter and dressing and result not only from disease but also from the techniques used, the spillage of contaminated matter, contact with the outer hide or skin of the slaughtered animals, regurgitated stomach contents, and faecal matter. Particular causes for concern include inadequately cleaned sticking knives and pithing rods, incorrect flaying, soiling of the carcase, and problems with the skinning and 'tailing-out' of animals dressed on the floors of slaughterhouses.

Few people, even committed vegetarians, would care to spend time in an abattoir; but one who has is Dr Alan Long:

> The gangs have always invited me to join in their tea-breaks, although I have never been offered clean overalls for my visits (the best advice I received: 'Bring old clothes: there's a lot of blood in there'). Hygiene is execrable. Bouts of idiotic and obscene chanting occur in the din . . . Many slaughtermen are defensive over their tasks ('Well it's legal, isn't it?'). Many declare their revulsion at killing calves and horses and at ritual slaughter ('But it's all part of the job, isn't it?'). Piece-work rates leave very little time for niceties.
>
> Vets and meat-inspectors harden in their attitudes . . . [One] managed, by tenuous recourse to hygiene regulations, to forestall a kill of fully conscious sheep by a slaughterman equipped with nothing more suitable than a blunt bread-knife.[9]

As a consequence of intensive methods of husbandry the meat producers have had to resort to the widespread use of antibiotics to counteract the disease-risks inherent in their methods. It is almost impossible to slaughter animals without substantial levels of contamination. Dr A. H. Linton of the Bristol University Medical School estimated that at least 52 per cent of bovine carcases and 83 per cent of pigs' carcases are contaminated by bacteria of the *E. coli* type, and there is an increasing spread of resistant bacteria and infections of the urinary tract, enteritis in babies, salmonella infections, and cystitis as a result of drug-resistant enteric bacteria. Jon Wynne-Tyson reminds us that

> Decomposition begins as soon as an animal is slaughtered. Its blood stream, just like our own, serves as a debris conveyor for toxic wastes . . . To give our system the additional job of eliminating another creature's unwanted material together with the toxins of fear that are released into its bloodstream prior to slaughter seems to suggest, at the very least, a very unaesthetic regard for the joys of nutrition.

Flesh foods are nearly always responsible for food poisoning. In 1975 there were 11,000 *reported* cases of salmonella poisoning in the UK. Three years later, in 1978, a report by the British Association for the Advancement of Science noted: 'Undoubtedly the greatest dangers arise from conditions in slaughterhouses. Contaminated meat is perhaps the main cause of the pathogen's spread.' This view received tragic confirmation in 1984 when nineteen old people died of food poisoning at the Stanley Royd Hospital in Yorkshire. There had been salmonella outbreaks at the hospital in 1974 and 1979, and in March 1982 mince had been returned from the wards as unacceptable: laboratory experiments showed that there would have been a real danger if this had been eaten. The 1984 salmonella contamination infected more than 400 patients and staff. It was originally thought that cold beef had been responsible for the contamination but the subsequent inquiry was told that, though beef may have been a vehicle, it was virtually certain that poultry had been the original source of the infection.

There are also indications that infection by beef tapeworms is increasing in the UK. Tapeworm infection was practically unknown before the Second World War, and even now it arouses little publicity because the worms actually do little physical damage to their human hosts, despite their horrific size. In 1978 two scientists, Dr William Crewe and Dr Roderick Owen, both of the Liverpool School of Tropical Medicine, published an article on beef tapeworms in *New Scientist*. Though the symptoms of beef tapeworm infection in humans are comparatively mild, even with worms that exceed forty feet, the situation is obviously not a desirable one. 'The implications are', said the article, 'that a considerable reservoir of tapeworm infection has already established itself in Britain.'

Meat, then, contains two broad categories of contaminants: those introduced by meat producers, such as growth boosters (hormones), antibiotics, and tranquillizers, and naturally occurring pollutants — the unavoidable by-products of animal metabolism, such as lactic and uric acid, neither of which are beneficial for humans (a high concentration of uric acid predisposes towards kidney stones, gout, and arthritis). Adrenaline and other hormones released into animals' bodies as a result of the terror induced by the slaughterhouse are also passed on to the human consumers of their dead flesh. The American researcher Orville Schell, whose four-year investigation resulted in a damning indictment of the meat and poultry industry in the USA, detailed in his book *Modern Meat*, reveals that nearly half of all antibiotics manufactured go into animals, and there is mounting evidence that resistance to antibiotics is being passed on to humans.

★   ★   ★

In the course of our brief survey we have skirted many profound and important issues, all of which have a bearing, whether we realize it or not, on the relatively simple decision to stop eating meat. Readers who wish to follow up some or all of the topics touched on in this book will find a number of suggestions for further study in the Reading List. It is important for vegetarians to be informed if they are to hold their own in a still predominantly carnivorous society, and if they are to stand any chance of persuading others that their dietary choice is both ethically and practically necessary.

How far, though, can one legitimately go in persuading other people to give up meat?

The hard-line approach is to assert that food habits cannot be left to personal whim or habit or the vagaries of market forces; that dietary good sense must, in some way or other, be made to prevail; that, in a word, the right to eat badly and immorally is not an inalienable right. The right to eat what one pleases, if what one pleases is the flesh of defenceless fellow creatures, is not an absolute one and if persisted in demands militant opposition at every opportunity.

A more moderate approach is to assume that, by and large, it is people's ignorance that enforces the meat habit, and that it is this that is the main stumbling block to a wider extension of vegetarianism. If people knew more about the realities of modern meat production, the argument might run, then they would make the right choices of their own volition.

This is the essence of what we called in the first edition of this book the subversive way: to place the right sort of information courteously but with firm persistence before people whenever we have the opportunity, in order to try and make them look at their traditional assumptions about what they eat in a new way. Everyone rightly suspects the blood and thunder preacher, with his purple prose and wagging finger, of humbug. Vehemence and militancy are often self-defeating. Gentler, more insidious, means are usually required.

Persuading your friends and neighbours to give up meat, it might be said, brings its own moral dilemma: is it ethical to force people into doing something that they don't want to do? It is, after all, a conflict of freedoms: the freedom of certain types of animals to live out their allotted span without being slaughtered for food by human beings, and the freedom of the human animal to eat what pleases him. For anyone who has considered the issues, even on a superficial level, the dilemma is a spurious one. There can be no question about it: the moral right of any creature to life — leaving aside for the moment all other considerations — is infinitely greater than the right of another creature to condemn it to live only for slaughter simply to gratify a perverted palate.

It is clear that people are changing their attitudes towards meat. At the time of writing there may be as many as 20 million people in the UK who have reduced their meat consumption over the past fifteen years, and the trend towards an avoidance of meat and outright vegetarianism is now of statistical significance. The meat trade certainly thinks so and is desperately trying to shore up its crumbling defences against the formidable logic of vegetarianism. Back in May 1977 the *Meat Trades Journal* was pointing to the kind of association meat producers do *not* want their customers to make: 'To acquaint the customer', it says, 'with the knowledge that the lamb chops she has just purchased were part of the anatomy of one of those pretty little creatures we see gambolling in the fields at springtime is probably the surest way of turning her into a vegetarian.' Though we may marvel at the cynicism, the reasoning is impeccable. When asked how she and Paul became vegetarians, Linda McCartney replied:

I never thought about it really until one day when we were having lunch at our farmhouse in Scotland. In the middle of the traditional Sunday roast, we noticed the lambs gambolling in the fields outside and it struck us that we were eating one of those lambs, that I was eating somebody's leg . . . Then, while we were on holiday in Barbados, of all places, we were driving along following a truck full of lovely hens when it turned into a chicken processing plant . . . Anyway, then we decided not to eat meat anymore and we haven't eaten it since.[10]

The meat trade relies on disassociation. It needs to keep the image of the animal in the field well away from the product it eventually becomes: the sausages and chops and rump steaks must in no way be linked to real pigs, real sheep, or real cows.

All kinds of people, not just vegetarians or animal rights activists, are shocked by organized dog fights for money, or horrified at the sight of a hare being ripped to pieces by greyhounds, or she-foxes savaged on a Saturday afternoon; and yet these same people feel nothing about the horrors that are being perpetrated every day in their local slaughterhouse. And why is there a moral difference between the export of live calves to Europe with its attendant cruelties and organized dog fights? Only, one supposes, that we don't eat dogs — at least, not knowingly.

The case of the New Forest ponies that hit the UK headlines in 1978 highlights this widespread confusion of values. 'Shoot Me, Not Pony, Pleads Hospital Girl' was one emotive headline. Gipsy, the horse that fourteen-year-old Kim Bowen kidnapped in a futile bid to save her from slaughter, tugged at a good many heart strings. In the wake of that story came the not altogether unexpected revelation that the best ponies and foals from the New Forest were being sold to be slaughtered — and then eaten by humans. Foal meat, said one enterprising trader, tastes very much like veal.

People were rightly disturbed and upset that the ponies were ending up on people's plates. In other words, they realized — or, perhaps more accurately, remembered — that living, breathing animals and 'meat' were not distinct, unrelated entities. But this is exactly what most people fail to do in the case of cows, sheep and pigs. Persuading people to make this identification should be the prime duty of all vegetarians. Why be shocked at the slaughter of pretty New Forest ponies, or hares, or foxes, when calves, lambs, cows, bullocks, sheep, and pigs undergo unspeakable suffering every single day?

But is a vegetarian diet feasible on a world, or even a national, scale? A common question put to vegetarians is, 'If everyone became a vegetarian, wouldn't all the animals now reared for meat die out, and wouldn't that be ethically unacceptable to vegetarians?'

Well, yes, if the changeover to national vegetarianism happened instantly, as if by legal decree, leaving us with countless thousands of redundant animals — not to mention redundant humans in the meat industry. But of course it would not happen like this. The process of dietary change would be a gradual one: after all, horses did not become extinct after the invention of the internal combustion engine. We can envisage a steady decline in the demand for meat, as well as for milk and eggs, that would oblige farmers to breed fewer animals and develop other means of making a living in the new climate of taste and opinion.

This scenario does not altogether dispose of the problem of redundant animals; but such animals are, to a large extent, human creations: they have been bred specifically to meet human requirements, reared in artificial environments, and subjected to suffering in the name of efficient husbandry, from mutilation to social deprivation. The case is not one involving wild animals in their natural habitat; it is one of developed breeds, manipulated and exploited by humans for their own purposes. Such creatures are bred 'in the full knowledge that their lives will be, at the least distorted and unnatural, at worst filled with pain and fear, and we do it solely because there's profit in the business'.[11] It is questionable whether any life is better than no life at all; for some animals, indeed, it can be argued strongly that it would have been better if they had never been born. When we consider the matter in this light, is it absolutely clear that the extinction of such breeds, if that is what it came to, would be a bad thing *for them?*

In any case, turning the land over to crop production for human rather than animal consumption would lead to a more varied and interesting landscape in which there would certainly be room for wild life parks for native breeds of livestock animals to roam in comparative freedom.

To the cynic this still sounds like a pipe-dream, and indeed we may never have to face the problem in this way. The present and the immediate future are of more importance, and it is here that every new vegetarian has a contribution to make in educating others so that the trend towards a reduction in meat consumption (beginning with red meats) will continue to grow and thus exert more pressure on meat interests. We may never be a totally vegetarian nation; in many ways that is an unworkable ideal; but we can certainly strive towards a time when the balance tips firmly in favour of a healthier and more humane way of eating, when, if animals are still eaten by humans, they are reared and killed using methods that cause the least possible suffering.

That time may be nearer than we think. A report in *The Guardian* in July 1984 described the reaction of the Meat Promotion Executive to Sarah Brown's 'Vegetarian Kitchen' series on BBC television. The

MPE was worried that vegetarianism would become respectable as a result of such a series, and that this would further encourage the trend towards meatless meals. 'What is highly likely', said a leader in the *Meat Trades Journal,* 'is that more and more people will try the recipes. And more and more people will find they enjoy what they are eating.' How terrible!

Worried by this subversive trend the MPE launched a six million pound campaign to put across 'a positive image for meat'. They do have something to worry about. In the UK, according to one poll, 25 per cent of the population now eat meat only occasionally, whilst 4 per cent (2.24 million) either avoid red meat or were outright vegetarians. 'Watch out,' warned the *Meat Trades Journal* in April 1984, 'the vegetarians are on the attack', whilst Colin Cullimore, addressing the International Beef Symposium in 1984, acknowledged the changing climate of opinion when he said: 'Feeding cereals to animals so that the affluent might eat meat was starving the poor in underdeveloped countries. Breeding and killing innocent animals just for the pleasure of eating them was cruel. These are some of the arguments put forward not by a cranky minority, but a growing vociferous and increasingly influential sector of the population.'[12]

In 1985 the first vegetarian catering course was offered in the UK, yet another small sign of the times. The prospectus for the course, at Plymouth College of Further Education, noted: 'Up until now there were no catering courses available . . . suitable for the vegetarians, vegans, wholefooders, or people from ethnic minorities with dietary restrictions. This meant literally millions of people in England were prevented from being trained for a career in this industry.'[13]

Vegetarians are also in the forefront of the increasingly sophisticated public awareness of environmental factors in health and disease. Here, too, scientific research is filtering down to affect everyday concerns. Vegetarians can only welcome developments such as the decision to offer a wholefood menu to the boys at the Dyson Hall Observation and Assessment Centre in Liverpool following the findings of the American researcher Alexander Schauss, whose book *Diet, Crime and Delinquency* pointed to food additives and refined foods as two key culprits in triggering what he termed 'anti-social behaviour' (someone should perhaps study the dietary patterns of football hooligans). We must not underestimate how much still needs to be accomplished. The vegetarian movement, rather like the peace movement, is hampered by lack of financial resources: it simply cannot afford to put its case over to the mass public as slickly and as powerfully as the vested interests associated with meat consumption. But a start, and a good one, may be said to have been made on changing public consciousness in relation to a non-meat diet.

Vegetarianism is not a weak-minded fad, a mere pose, or a cosily sentimental feeling for animals. On the contrary, it is, or should be, a lifelong commitment, a lifestyle anchored on firm moral and intellectual convictions, a responsible acknowledgement that our species, for all its wonderful and unique gifts, is only one of many with no absolute right to dispose of non-human animals and the environments in which they live merely in order to satisfy a culinary whim. That whim has already been the death of countless millions of animals, and, indirectly, of many human beings. It is time we grew up. There are signs that we are beginning to do so. With every new vegetarian the world takes one small step towards sanity.

5.

RECIPES

SIMPLE, easy to prepare, and nourishing. These are the main features of the following selection of recipes, which have been chosen to provide a basic 'starter-pack' of meal ideas for vegetarian soups, starters, and main meals that will fit in with busy modern lifestyles.

The recipes are also aimed at those who wish to reduce their meat consumption by replacing a few meat meals a week with vegetarian dishes. All the recipes use familiar, easy to obtain ingredients, which should help both new vegetarians and meat reducers to ease themselves into the habit of going without meat.

A few points to keep in mind:

Cheese. Most cheeses are made with rennet, which comes from calves. Wherever possible, therefore, vegetarians should only eat non-rennet (vegetarian) cheeses, of which more and more are coming on to the market. These are readily available in most supermarkets. Genetic engineers have recently produced rennin (an enzyme from the fourth stomach of an unweaned calf) from bacteria, which opens up the prospect of cheaper non-rennet products for vegetarians. Though vegetarian cheeses have not been specified in the recipes they should be used wherever possible.

Stock. Remember always to use vegetable stock, either bought or prepared at home (see p. 93).

For general health reasons, *flour* should normally be 100 per cent wholemeal (wholewheat), 81 per cent at the lowest.

Sugar should be raw cane sugar.

Seasonings should be sea salt and freshly-ground black pepper.

Fats and oils should be vegetable in origin (e.g. corn oil), margarine should be polyunsaturated (lard and suet are animal-derived and high in saturated fats).

Rice should be brown.

Gelatin, made from animal bones, is to be avoided. Use agar-agar or carrageen instead.

Remember that Worcester Sauce contains anchovies. Vegetarian varieties (e.g. Holbrooks) are available.

Throughout the recipes, servings are for four people.

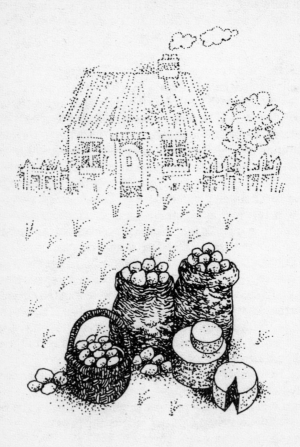

Soups, Starters and Salads

A good soup is a meal in itself, complemented by fresh wholemeal (wholewheat) bread and a side salad. Soups can be prepared in advance and even taken to work in a flask as a counter to the temptation of fast food lunches. They are also ideal for those who have to snatch quick lunches at home, being filling and nourishing without blowing you out for the rest of the afternoon!

BASIC VEGETABLE STOCK

Green vegetable water, which can be saved and stored in the refrigerator, makes excellent basic stock. If you need to make up some stock, simply dissolve a teaspoon of Marmite/yeast extract in ¾ pint (425ml/2 cups) of warm water. Alternatively, vegetable stock cubes are readily available.

BASIC VEGETABLE SOUP

Imperial (Metric)	American
½ lb (225g) fresh tomatoes	½ pound fresh tomatoes
1 large onion	1 large onion
1 carrot	1 carrot
1 small swede	1 small rutabaga
1 turnip	1 turnip
1 medium-sized potato	1 medium-sized potato
1 medium-sized parsnip	1 medium-sized parsnip
1 tablespoon polyunsaturated margarine	1 tablespoon polyunsaturated margarine
1½ pints (850ml) vegetable stock	3¾ cups vegetable stock
2 oz (55g) wholemeal macaroni, spaghetti, or noodles	½ cup wholewheat macaroni, spaghetti, or noodles
4 oz (115g) red kidney beans (cooked)	¾ cup red kidney beans (cooked)
1 teaspoon Marmite/yeast extract	1 teaspoon yeast extract
Grated cheese to garnish	Grated cheese to garnish

1. Peel and prepare all the vegetables and chop them into even-sized pieces.

2. Melt the margarine in a saucepan and sauté the onion for a few minutes.

3. Add the carrot, followed by the swede (rutabaga) and the turnip, and continue to cook gently for 2-3 minutes. Finally, add the potato and the parsnip.

4. Cover with the stock and season as desired with sea salt and freshly-ground black pepper.

5. Add the chopped tomatoes. Cover and cook slowly until all the vegetables are tender (about 30 minutes).

6. Add the pasta of your choice, the cooked kidney beans, and the Marmite/yeast extract. Cook for a further 10-15 minutes.

7. Serve with grated cheese of your choice.

EASY VEGETABLE SOUP

Imperial (Metric)
A few outer cabbage leaves
2 large carrots
½ lb (225g) potatoes
1 medium-sized onion
3 sticks celery
1½ oz (45g) polyunsaturated
  margarine
1½ pints (850ml) basic vegetable
  stock
½ teaspoon marjoram
2 teaspoons Marmite or yeast
  extract
Sea salt/freshly ground black pepper
Grated cheese to garnish

American
A few outer cabbage leaves
2 large carrots
½ pound potatoes
1 medium-sized onion
3 stalks celery
3 tablespoons polyunsaturated
  margarine
3¾ cups basic vegetable stock
½ teaspoon marjoram
2 teaspoons yeast extract
Sea salt/freshly ground black pepper
Grated cheese to garnish

1. Cut the cabbage leaves into narrow strips. Peel and cube the carrots, potatoes, onion, and celery.

2. Melt the margarine in a heavy-based saucepan. Sauté the carrots for a few minutes, and then add the celery followed by the cabbage and the onion.

3. Cover and cook gently for about 10 minutes, stirring occasionally.

4. Add the potatoes and cook for a further 5 minutes. Then add ½ pint (285ml/1⅓ cups) of basic vegetable stock and cook until the vegetables are nearly tender.

5. Add the rest of the stock, together with the marjoram, Marmite or yeast extract, and seasonings to taste. Cook for 5 minutes.

6. Serve sprinkled liberally with grated cheese of your choice.

CREAM OF SPINACH SOUP

Imperial (Metric)

½ lb (225g) chopped spinach
1 large onion
2 oz (55g) polyunsaturated
  margarine
2 oz (55g) wholemeal flour
1 pint (570ml) basic vegetable stock
1 pint (570ml) milk
Sea salt to taste
Grated nutmeg

American

1 cup chopped spinach
1 large onion
¼ cup polyunsaturated
  margarine
½ cup wholewheat flour
2½ cups basic vegetable stock
2½ cups milk
Sea salt to taste
Grated nutmeg

1. Cook the chopped spinach.

2. Peel and cut the onion up finely and sauté in the margarine until it is golden brown.

3. Add the flour and cook for 5 minutes, stirring all the time.

4. Add the stock and the milk and cook for a further 10 minutes.

5. Add the cooked spinach, sea salt, and a pinch of grated nutmeg.

LENTIL SOUP

Imperial (Metric)

2 oz (55g) lentils
1 large onion
1 carrot
1 clove of garlic
1 teaspoon wholemeal flour
¼ pint (140ml) milk
Sea salt and freshly ground black
  pepper to season

American

2 cups lentils
1 large onion
1 carrot
1 clove of garlic
1 teaspoon wholewheat flour
⅔ cup milk
Sea salt and freshly ground black
  pepper to season

1. Rinse the lentils in cold water and then soak them in ¾ pint (425ml/2 cups) of boiling water for an hour.

2. Bring back to the boil and skim.

3. Add the peeled and sliced onion, carrot, and garlic clove.

4. Simmer for about an hour and then pass soup through a sieve or put into a blender.

5. Thicken with the flour that has been blended with the milk.

6. Season, reheat, and serve.

POTATO AND LEEK SOUP

Imperial (Metric)	American
1 large onion	1 large onion
2 medium-sized leeks	2 medium-sized leeks
1 tablespoon polyunsaturated margarine	1 tablespoon polyunsaturated margarine
2 large potatoes	2 large potatoes
1½ pints (850ml) vegetable stock	3¾ cups vegetable stock
Sea salt and freshly ground black pepper to season	Sea salt and freshly ground black pepper to season
Top of the milk (if needed)	Top of the milk (if needed)
Single cream	Light cream
Parsley or watercress to garnish	Parsley or watercress to garnish

1. Slice the onion and the leeks and sauté in the margarine in a large saucepan, taking care they do not brown.

2. Peel, dice, and add the potatoes.

3. Cover the saucepan and cook gently for about 5 minutes.

4. Add the vegetable stock and the seasonings and simmer until the potatoes are tender.

5. Liquidize the soup, or put through a sieve. If the soup is too thick, add top of the milk as necessary. *Chill if desired.*

6. Serve with a swirl of single cream and garnish with freshly-chopped parsley or watercress.

CHILLED CARROT SOUP

Imperial (Metric)	American
1 medium-sized onion	1 medium-sized onion
3 garlic cloves	3 garlic cloves
1¼ lb (565g) young carrots	1¼ pounds young carrots
1½ pints (850ml) vegetable stock	3¾ cups vegetable stock
⅓ pint (200ml) double cream	¾ cup heavy cream
Sea salt and freshly ground black pepper to season	Sea salt and freshly ground black pepper to season
Parsley to garnish	Parsley to garnish

1. Peel and thinly slice the onion and garlic cloves.

2. Melt the margarine in a saucepan and add the onion and the garlic. Cook over a low heat, keeping the pan covered, until the onion is soft and transparent.

3. Meanwhile, scrape the carrots and chop them thinly.

4. Add the carrots to the onion and garlic and cook for about 8 minutes.

5. Add the stock and simmer for a further 30 minutes.

6. Allow to cool and then liquidize or sieve until smooth.

7. When the soup is cool, add the cream, sea salt and black pepper as required. Chill for at least an hour before serving.

8. Garnish with chopped parsley and a swirl of cream.

WATERCRESS SOUP

Imperial (Metric)	American
1 medium-sized onion	1 medium-sized onion
4 medium-sized potatoes	4 medium-sized potatoes
2 oz (55g) polyunsaturated margarine	¼ cup polyunsaturated margarine
5 bunches watercress	5 bunches watercress
Sea salt and freshly ground black pepper	Sea salt and freshly ground black pepper
1 pint (570ml) milk	2½ cups milk

1. Slice the onion and peel and quarter the potatoes.

2. Melt 1 oz (30g/2 tablespoons) of the margarine in a saucepan. Add the onion and potatoes.

3. Cover and cook gently over a low heat for about 10 minutes, making sure that the vegetables do not brown.

4. Clean and strip the leaves from 4 bunches of watercress. Add to the onion and potatoes.

5. Add sea salt and black pepper as required, and enough water to cover the ingredients. Cover the pan and cook until the potatoes are tender.

6. Add the milk and the remaining bunch of watercress. Cook for a further 5 minutes.

7. Liquidize or sieve the soup and reheat, adding the remaining margarine and a squeeze of lemon juice if desired. Chill at this point if desired.

FRENCH ONION SOUP

Imperial (Metric)
¾ lb (340g) onions
2 oz (55g) polyunsaturated margarine
1 tablespoon wholemeal flour
2 pints (1¼ litres) warm water
1 teaspoon Marmite/yeast extract
Sea salt and freshly ground black pepper
1 tablespoon red wine

American
¾ pound onions
¼ cup polyunsaturated margarine
1 tablespoon wholewheat flour
5 cups warm water
1 teaspoon yeast extract
Sea salt and freshly ground black pepper
1 tablespoon red wine

1. Peel and slice the onions and drop them into a saucepan in which the margarine has been melted. Make sure that the pan is really hot and shake well so that the onions are nicely coated with the melted margarine. Adjust the heat so that the onions brown gently, but be careful not to let them blacken.

2. Stir in the flour until this too is browned (about 4 minutes).

3. Take off the heat and very gradually add the warm water into which the Marmite/yeast extract has been dissolved. This must be done carefully to avoid lumpiness.

4. Bring to the boil.

5. Add the sea salt and black pepper and allow to simmer with the lid on for 20 minutes. Just before serving add the tablespoon of red wine, but do not reheat after this or the wine will turn bitter.

5. Serve with croûtons of toasted cheese squares.

CHESTNUT SOUP

Imperial (Metric)
1 oz (30g) polyunsaturated
   margarine
½ lb (225g) chestnuts
1 medium-sized onion
2 oz (55g) celery
1 small carrot
½ pint (285ml) vegetable stock
¼ teaspoon sea salt
¼ teaspoon raw cane sugar
Sprig of thyme and parsley
½ pint (285ml) creamy milk

American
2½ tablespoons polyunsaturated
   margerine
½ pound chestnuts
1 medium-sized onion
½ cup celery
1 small carrot
1⅓ cups vegetable stock
¼ teaspoon sea salt
¼ teaspoon raw cane sugar
Sprig of thyme and parsley
1⅓ cups creamy milk

1. Melt the margarine in a heavy pan (skillet).

2. Shell the chestnuts and slice the vegetables thinly. Add all these
    to the melted margarine and leave to brown slightly before adding
    the heated stock, sea salt, raw cane sugar, and the herbs.

3. Allow to simmer for an hour and then strain the liquid into a
    bowl and press the chestnuts and the vegetables through a sieve.

4. Pour the liquid back over the chestnut and vegetable purée,
    stirring all the time. Simmer for 5 minutes.

5. Just before serving, add the creamy milk and top with parsley.

GREEK MUSHROOMS

Imperial (Metric)	**American**
1½ lb (680g) button mushrooms	1½ pounds button mushrooms
4 spring onions	4 scallions
2 garlic cloves	2 garlic cloves
½ pint (285ml) red wine vinegar	1⅓ cups red wine vinegar
Juice of 1 lemon	Juice of 1 lemon
2 tablespoons raw cane sugar	2 tablespoons raw cane sugar
Small bunch of parsley	Small bunch of parsley
Bouquet garni	Bouquet garni
4 tablespoons olive oil	4 tablespoons olive oil
Sea salt and freshly ground black pepper to season	Sea salt and freshly ground black pepper to season

1. Wash the mushrooms, pat dry, and remove and discard the stalks.

2. Chop the spring onions (scallions). Peel and chop the garlic.

3. In a saucepan, bring the red wine vinegar, lemon juice, raw cane sugar, spring onions (scallions), garlic, parsley, and bouquet garni to the boil. Cover and simmer for 20 minutes.

4. Strain the liquid and then return it to the saucepan. Add the olive oil, mushrooms and seasoning. Simmer for about 5 minutes.

5. Cool and leave to marinate overnight if possible.

6. Serve chilled in small individual dishes sprinkled with chopped parsley.

BRUSSELS SPROUT PATÉ

Imperial (Metric)	American
½ lb (225g) Brussels sprouts	½ pound Brussels sprouts
4 oz (115g) wholemeal bread (without crusts)	¼ pound wholewheat bread (without crusts)
2 tablespoons lemon juice	2 tablespoons lemon juice
3 tablespoons sunflower oil	3 tablespoons sunflower oil
2 tablespoons olive oil	2 tablespoons olive oil
1 teaspoon freshly grated nutmeg	1 teaspoon freshly grated nutmeg
Dash of Tabasco sauce	Dash of Tabasco sauce
Sea salt and freshly ground black pepper to taste	Sea salt and freshly ground black pepper to taste
Paprika and chopped parsley to garnish	Paprika and chopped parsley to garnish

1. Wash and prepare the sprouts. Cook in boiling salted water for about 10 minutes until just tender and still bright green. Strain and leave to cool.

2. Dip the bread into a little water until soft. Squeeze out excess water.

3. Put the sprouts, bread, lemon juice, and oils into a food processor or liquidizer and blend until smooth. Season with the nutmeg, Tabasco, sea salt, and black pepper.

4. Put into individual dishes and chill. Garnish before serving with paprika and parsley. Serve with wholemeal (wholewheat) toast, crusty bread, or pitta bread.

LEEK AND TOMATO STARTER

Imperial (Metric)	American
6 medium-sized leeks	6 medium-sized leeks
1 small onion	1 small onion
6 tomatoes	6 tomatoes
4 tablespoons olive oil	4 tablespoons olive oil
1 garlic clove	1 garlic clove
¼ pint (140ml) dry white wine	⅔ cup dry white wine
1 bouquet garni	1 bouquet garni
Sea salt and freshly ground black pepper to season	Sea salt and freshly ground black pepper to season

1. Wash the leeks and cut them into pieces about 1½ inches long.

2. Peel and chop the onion. Skin the tomatoes.

3. Heat the olive oil in a saucepan. Add the leeks, onion, tomatoes and garlic. Sauté for a few minutes.

4. Add the white wine and bouquet garni. Cover the ingredients with water and add seasoning.

5. Cover the pan and simmer very gently for about 30 minutes, until the leeks are tender. Remove from heat and allow to cool. Remove bouquet garni.

6. Serve with crusty wholemeal (wholewheat) bread.

AVOCADO RICE SALAD

Imperial (Metric)	American
½ lb (225g) brown rice	1 cup brown rice
2 avocados	2 avocados
2 oz (55g) mushrooms	1 cup mushrooms
3 medium-sized tomatoes	3 medium-sized tomatoes
3 spring onions	3 scallions
2 hard-boiled eggs	2 hard-boiled eggs
Approx. ¼ pint (140ml) French dressing	Approx. ⅔ cup French dressing

1. Cook the rice until tender, then drain it and leave to cool.

2. Peel and stone the avocados, then cut them into cubes.

3. Wash and chop the mushrooms, tomatoes and spring onions (scallions), then peel and chop the eggs.

4. Put the rice into a deep salad bowl, add the avocado, mushrooms, eggs, tomatoes and onions and mix them gently.

5. Pour the dressing over the ingredients and mix it in thoroughly. Chill well.

PASTA AND BEANSPROUT SALAD

Imperial (Metric)	American
4 oz (115g) wholemeal noodles	1 cup wholewheat noodles
7 tablespoons sunflower oil	½ cup sunflower oil
1 bunch of watercress	1 bunch of watercress
3 cups beansprouts	3¾ cups beansprouts
2 tomatoes	2 tomatoes
3 oz (85g) cashew nuts, chopped and toasted	⅔ cup cashew nuts, chopped and toasted
1 oz (30g) wheatgerm, toasted	¼ cup wheatgerm toasted
1 oz (30g) sesame seeds, toasted	2½ tablespoons sesame seeds, toasted
6 tablespoons lemon juice	½ cup lemon juice
Seasoning to taste	Seasoning to taste

1. Cook the noodles until tender. Drain them well, place them in a bowl and mix in 1 tablespoonful of the sunflower oil. Set aside to chill.

2. Wash, trim and drain the watercress, the beansprouts, and chop the tomatoes finely.

3. Arrange the noodles around the outside of a large serving platter, followed by a ring of watercress, then a ring of beansprouts, finishing off with a ring of tomatoes and chopped nuts in the centre.

4. Mix the wheatgerm, sesame seeds, lemon juice, oil and seasoning together and pour the dressing over the salad.

CHICK PEA (GARBANZO) SALAD

Imperial (Metric)	American
6 oz (170g) dried chick peas	¾ cup dried garbanzo beans
1 small onion	1 small onion
½ small clove garlic	½ small clove garlic
Juice of 1 lemon	Juice of 1 lemon
2 dessertspoons olive oil	2 tablespoons olive oil
½ teaspoon sea salt	½ teaspoon sea salt
Cayenne pepper	Cayenne pepper
3 tablespoons finely chopped parsley	3½ tablespoons finely chopped parsley

1. Soak the chick peas overnight in enough cold water to cover them. In the morning, drain the peas and put them in a saucepan covered with cold water. Simmer the peas for about 1½ hours, topping up with more cold water when necessary. Drain them and allow to cool.

2. Peel and chop the onion and garlic finely.

3. Mix together the lemon juice, olive oil, garlic, salt and cayenne pepper.

4. Put the peas and the chopped onion into a bowl, pour the dressing over them and mix thoroughly. Chill well before serving, garnished with parsley.

SALAD ROULADE

Imperial (Metric)	American
½ Webbs lettuce	½ Webbs lettuce
2 tomatoes	2 tomatoes
1 oz (30g) mushrooms	½ cup mushrooms
2 small spring onions	2 small scallions
A little Parmesan cheese, grated	A little Parmesan cheese, grated
6 oz (170g) grated cheese	1½ cups grated cheese
2 oz (55g) fresh wholemeal breadcrumbs	1 cup fresh wholewheat breadcrumbs

4 eggs (free range)
¼ pint (140ml) single cream
Seasoning to taste
1 teaspoon ready-made mustard
2 tablespoons warm water
4 tablespoons mayonnaise
Parsley to garnish

4 eggs (free range)
⅔ cup light cream
Seasoning to taste
1 teaspoon ready-made mustard
2 tablespoons warm water
4 tablespoons mayonnaise
Parsley to garnish

1. Heat the oven to 400°F/200°C (Gas Mark 6).

2. Wash and dry the lettuce and shred it finely, then wash and slice the tomatoes and mushrooms thinly. Chop the spring onions (scallions).

3. Line a Swiss roll tin (approximately 13 × 9 inches/33 × 23cm) with greaseproof paper and sprinkle with the grated Parmesan.

4. Mix the grated cheese and breadcrumbs together in a bowl.

5. Separate the eggs and add the yolks to the cheese and breadcrumb mixture. Also add the cream, seasoning and mustard and stir in the warm water to make a fairly soft mixture.

6. Whisk the egg whites until they form peaks and fold them carefully into the mixture.

7. Spread the mixture carefully onto the Swiss roll tin and bake it for 10-15 minutes until it rises and is firm to the touch.

8. Allow it to cool slightly and then place a clean, damp tea-towel over the top until absolutely cold.

9. Sprinkle a sheet of greaseproof paper generously with grated Parmesan. Loosen the edges of the roulade and tip it gently on to the paper.

10. Spread the roulade with mayonnaise and then lay the sliced mushrooms, onions and tomatoes on top. Season well and using the greaseproof paper, roll the roulade up as you would a Swiss roll. Lay it on a plate and garnish with chopped parsley. Serve the roulade cut into slices.

Vegetable Dishes

There are two golden rules to observe when cooking all vegetables: do not oversoak, and do not overcook. In fact, as regards the first, it is best not to soak at all. Gentle washing, steaming or, better still, sautéing are much better.

In meat cookery, vegetables are relegated to side positions. Here are some vegetarian recipes that make them the centre of attraction.

VEGETABLE CHOP SUEY

Imperial (Metric)	American
2 large carrots	2 large carrots
2 large onions	2 large onions
2/3 sticks of celery	2/3 stalks of celery
½ head of cabbage	½ head of cabbage
3 tablespoons vegetable oil	3 tablespoons vegetable oil
¾ pint (425ml) vegetable stock	2 cups vegetable stock
2 tablespoons soya sauce	2 tablespoons soy sauce
½ teaspoon yeast extract	½ teaspoon yeast extract
2 teaspoons wholemeal flour	2 teaspoons wholewheat flour
4 tablespoons water	4 tablespoons water
½ lb (225g) fresh bean sprouts	½ pound fresh bean sprouts
½ lb (225g) brown rice	½ pound brown rice
Sea salt to season	Sea salt to season

1. Peel and slice the carrots and the onions.

2. Cut the celery and the cabbage into inch-long pieces.

3. Heat the vegetable oil in a heavy-based saucepan (a Chinese wok is best). Add the vegetables, and stir well so that they are covered by the oil. Cover and cook for 3 minutes.

4. Add the vegetable stock and simmer for a further 3 minutes. Add the soya (soy) sauce and yeast extract.

5. Blend the flour and water and add to the vegetables. Cook gently for 5 minutes.

6. Add the bean sprouts. Stir thoroughly and add some more stock (or water) if the mixture is too thick. Serve with the brown rice.

Remember: It is absolutely essential not to overcook the vegetables.

VEGETABLE CURRY

Imperial (Metric)	**American**
1 large onion	1 large onion
1 small cauliflower	1 small cauliflower
3 or 4 medium-sized potatoes	3 or 4 medium-sized potatoes
2 medium-sized carrots	2 medium-sized carrots
3 tablespoons vegetable oil	3 tablespoons vegetable oil
2 oz (55g) wholemeal flour	½ cup wholewheat flour
1 tablespoon curry powder	1 tablespoon curry powder
¾ pint (425ml) coconut stock (see point 6)	2 cups coconut stock (see point 6)
Sea salt and freshly ground black pepper	Sea salt and freshly ground black pepper
2 tablespoons lemon juice	2 tablespoons lemon juice

1. Peel and chop the onion and break the cauliflower into florettes.

2. Peel and dice the potatoes and slice the carrots.

3. Heat a little of the oil in a large heavy-based saucepan. Add the onion and fry until well browned.

4. Add the flour and cook for a few moments, then add the curry powder.

5. Put in the rest of the prepared vegetables and stir well, making sure that the mixture is well covered with curry and oil. Cover the pan and sauté for 5 minutes.

6. Make the coconut stock by seeping 3 oz (85g/1 cup) desiccated coconut in ¾ pint (425ml/2 cups) boiling water for 15 minutes. Pour the strained stock over the vegetables.

7. Season and allow to simmer gently until the vegetables are tender. Add the lemon juice just before serving.

Note: Curries are best prepared early in the day, or even during the previous one, and left to allow the flavours to mingle and be thoroughly absorbed. However, reheat carefully to avoid breaking up the vegetables.

FRUITY CURRY

Imperial (Metric)	American
½ lb (225g) split peas	½ pound split peas
½ lb (225g) brown rice	½ pound brown rice
2 medium-sized onions	2 medium-sized onions
2 large cooking apples	2 large cooking apples
2 bananas	2 bananas
1 tablespoon curry powder	1 tablespoon curry powder
1 clove of garlic	1 clove of garlic
2 oz (55g) raisins/sultanas	⅔ cup raisins/golden seedless raisins
1 teaspoon lemon juice	1 teaspoon lemon juice
1 tablespoon chutney	1 tablespoon chutney
Sea salt and freshly ground black pepper	Sea salt and freshly ground black pepper
1 oz (30g) desiccated coconut	⅓ cup desiccated coconut

1. Wash the split peas and soak them overnight in the refrigerator (this will shorten the cooking time).

2. Cook the brown rice in a tightly-covered pan for 45 minutes and then keep warm.

3. Strain the split peas. Put into a saucepan and cover with boiling water. Boil until soft (about ¾ hour).

4. Add the chopped and peeled onions, apples and bananas, curry powder, garlic, and raisins/sultanas (golden seedless raisins). Simmer for a further ¼ hour, and then strain.

5. Add the lemon juice, chutney, and seasonings. Turn onto a hot serving dish, sprinkle with coconut, and surround with the cooked brown rice.

PARSNIP PIE

Imperial (Metric)	American
2 lb (900g) parsnips	2 pounds parsnips
1 lb (455g) tomatoes	1 pound tomatoes
Sea salt and freshly ground black pepper	Sea salt and freshly ground black pepper
3 oz (85g) raw cane sugar	½ cup raw cane sugar
¼ pint (140ml) single cream	⅔ cup light cream
6 oz (170g) grated Cheddar cheese	1¼ cups grated Cheddar cheese
1 cup wholemeal breadcrumbs	⅔ cup wholewheat breadcrumbs
3 oz (85g) polyunsaturated margarine	⅓ cup polyunsaturated margarine

1. Peel the parsnips and remove any hard cores. Slice thinly and fry lightly in a little olive oil for about 4 minutes.

2. Slice the tomatoes.

3. Grease an ovenproof dish and lay a layer of sliced parsnips in it. Sprinkle with sea salt, black pepper, a little raw cane sugar, and cream.

4. Cover with a layer of sliced tomatoes. Sprinkle with grated cheese and repeat these layers, finishing with the tomatoes and cheese.

5. Sprinkle breadcrumbs on the top and dot with margarine, sea salt, and black pepper. Cook for about 40 minutes at 325°F/170°C (Gas Mark 3) in the centre of the oven.

COURGETTES (ZUCCHINI) RICCIONI

Imperial (Metric)	American
1 lb (455g) courgettes	1 pound zucchini
1 large onion	1 large onion
1 oz (30g) polyunsaturated margarine	2½ tablespoons polyunsaturated margarine
3 eggs (free range)	3 eggs (free range)
1 teaspoon top milk	1 teaspoon top milk
Sea salt and black pepper	Sea salt and black pepper
Pinch of mixed herbs	Pinch of mixed herbs

1. Wash the courgettes (zucchini) and slice them lengthways into thin strips. Chop them finely.

2. Peel and dice the onion and fry gently in the margarine with the courgettes (zucchini) until they become a light golden-brown.

3. Beat the eggs with the milk. Add sea salt and black pepper (freshly ground) to taste, and a pinch of mixed herbs.

4. Pour the egg and milk mixture over the browned onions and courgettes (zucchini). Leave on a low heat until the eggs are set.

5. Brown the top under a hot grill and garnish with parsley.

STUFFED ONIONS

Imperial (Metric)
4 large Spanish onions
2 tablespoons wholemeal
   breadcrumbs
2 oz (55g) grated Cheddar cheese
2 oz (55g) polyunsaturated
   margarine
1 tablespoon chopped mixed nuts
Made mustard to taste
Sea salt and freshly ground black
   pepper

American
4 large Spanish onions
2 tablespoons wholewheat
   breadcrumbs
½ cup grated Cheddar cheese
¼ cup polyunsaturated margarine
1 tablespoon chopped mixed nuts
Made mustard to taste
Sea salt and freshly ground black
   pepper

1. Peel the onions but do not cut off the bases. Boil them gently for about ½ an hour until the outsides are tender. Lift them carefully out of the water and allow to cool.

2. Carefully remove the centres, chop them finely, and add them to a mixture of the breadcrumbs, cheese, margarine, nuts, and seasonings.

3. Fill each cavity with the mixture and place on a well-greased baking tray. Cook for about an hour, at 325°F/170°C (Gas Mark 3), or until browned.

TIAN OF ONION

Imperial (Metric)	American
½ lb (225g) wholemeal breadcrumbs	4 cups wholewheat breadcrumbs
5 tablespoons olive oil	5 tablespoons olive oil
3 lb (1.3 kilos) onions	3 pounds onions
2 oz (55g) wholemeal flour	½ cup wholewheat flour
⅓ pint (200ml) milk	¾ cup milk
Nutmeg	Nutmeg
Sea salt and freshly ground black pepper	Sea salt and freshly ground black pepper

1. Brown the breadcrumbs in 1 tablespoon of olive oil.

2. Peel and slice the onions and cook in boiling salted water until tender. Drain, but keep the liquid.

3. Make a sauce using the remainder of the olive oil blended with the flour. Gradually add a little milk and about ⅓ pint (200ml/ ¾ cup) of the onion liquid so that the sauce becomes the consistency of double (heavy) cream. Season with sea salt, black pepper, and nutmeg.

4. Grease an ovenproof dish lightly with olive oil and pour in just under half of the sauce. Cover with the cooked onion slices.

5. Pour the remaining sauce on top and sprinkle with the browned breadcrumbs.

6. Bake in the oven for about ½ an hour at 300°F/150°C (Gas Mark 2) until it is well browned.

SPICED LENTILS

Imperial (Metric)
1 medium-sized onion
1 large garlic clove
1 teaspoon ground coriander
½ teaspoon ground ginger
½ teaspoon ground cumin
¼ teaspoon ground chilli
¼ teaspoon ground turmeric
½ teaspoon sea salt
½ lb (225g) lentils
2 oz (55g) polyunsaturated
  margarine
1½ pints (850ml) water

American
1 medium-sized onion
1 large garlic clove
1 teaspoon ground coriander
½ teaspoon ground ginger
½ teaspoon ground cumin
¼ teaspoon ground chili
¼ teaspoon ground turmeric
½ teaspoon sea salt
1 cup lentils
¼ cup polyunsaturated margarine
3¾ cups water

1. Peel and chop the onion and then sauté gently in the margarine.

2. Crush the garlic and mix with the rest of the spices.

3. Wash and drain the lentils and add to the sautéed onion. Cook gently for 5 minutes, stirring occasionally.

4. Pour the 1½ pints (850ml/3¾ cups) of hot water over the mixture. Cover and allow to simmer for ½ an hour, or until the lentils are soft. Add more seasonings if required.

SAVOURY LENTIL ROAST

Imperial (Metric)	American
½ lb (225g) lentils	1 cup lentils
1 medium-sized onion	1 medium-sized onion
2 oz (55g) polyunsaturated margarine	¼ cup polyunsaturated margarine
1 bayleaf	1 bayleaf
½ pint (285ml) water	1⅓ cups water
1 teaspoon yeast extract	1 teaspoon yeast extract
2 eggs (free range)	2 eggs (free range)
1 clove of garlic	1 clove of garlic
3 oz (85g) cooked brown rice	½ cup cooked brown rice
6 oz (170g) grated Cheddar cheese	1¼ cups grated Cheddar cheese
4 oz (115g) wholemeal breadcrumbs	1 cup wholewheat breadcrumbs
Freshly ground black pepper to taste	Freshly ground black pepper to taste

1. Wash and soak the lentils for ¾ hour in boiling water.

2. Peel and chop the onion and sauté in the margarine.

3. Put the strained lentils into a large saucepan with the bayleaf and the ½ pint (285ml/1⅓ cups) of water. Bring to the boil and simmer for ¾ hour.

4. Remove the bayleaf and stir in the yeast extract.

5. Beat the eggs, crush the garlic clove, and combine all the ingredients.

6. Pack the mixture into a greased loaf tin and cook for 30 minutes at 300°F/150°C (Gas Mark 2).

7. Serve hot with a thick gravy made with vegetable stock thickened with wholemeal (wholewheat) flour and browned and seasoned with yeast extract.

CAULIFLOWER CHEESE

Imperial (Metric)
1 medium-sized cauliflower
2 oz (55g) polyunsaturated
   margarine
2 oz (55g) wholemeal flour
½ pint (285ml) milk
4 oz (115g) grated cheese
Sea salt and freshly ground black
   pepper

American
1 medium-sized cauliflower
¼ cup polyunsaturated margarine
½ cup wholewheat flour
1⅓ cups milk
1 cup grated cheese
Sea salt and freshly ground black
   pepper

1. Cook the cauliflower florettes in boiling salted water until they are tender. Meanwhile, make a cheese sauce by melting the margarine and flour, adding the milk gradually, and then bringing to the boil. Simmer for a few minutes, then add the cheese, reserving a little to add to the top of the cauliflower.

2. Add seasonings to the sauce, stir well, and cook until the cheese has melted.

3. Drain the cauliflower and place in an ovenproof dish.

4. Pour the sauce over it and sprinkle the top with the remaining cheese.

Note: This recipe can also be used for macaroni cheese by substituting 4 oz (115g/1 cup) of uncooked macaroni for the cauliflower.

BEAN AND SWEETCORN BAKE

Imperial (Metric)
½ lb (225g) cooked red kidney
  beans
4 oz (115g) sweetcorn
Sea salt and freshly ground black
  pepper
2 tomatoes
1 onion, finely chopped
1 hard-boiled egg (free range)
½ pint (285ml) cheese sauce (page
  117)
Grated cheese for garnish

American
1¼ cups cooked red kidney beans
¾ cup sweetcorn
Sea salt and freshly ground black
  pepper
2 tomatoes
1 onion, finely chopped
1 hard-boiled egg (free range)
1⅓ cups cheese sauce (page 117)
Grated cheese for garnish

1. Mix the beans and the sweetcorn together and add sea salt and black pepper to taste.

2. Place in a casserole dish and lay slices of tomato and hard-boiled egg over the top. Sprinkle with the chopped onion.

3. Pour the cheese sauce over and sprinkle with grated cheese.

4. Cook for about 40 minutes at 350°F/180°C (Gas Mark 4).

SPINACH MOUSSE

Imperial (Metric)
1 lb (455g) fresh spinach
6 oz (170g) polyunsaturated
  margarine
Sea salt and freshly ground black
  pepper
¼ pint (140ml) double cream
2 oz (55g) wholemeal flour
3 fl oz (90ml) milk
4 eggs (free range)

American
1 pound fresh spinach
⅔ cup polyunsaturated margarine
Sea salt and freshly ground black
  pepper
⅔ cup heavy cream
½ cup wholewheat flour
⅓ cup milk
4 eggs (free range)

1. Wash and pick over the spinach and cook with 1 oz (30g/2½ tablespoons) of margarine (there is no need to use any water) for about 5 minutes. Add 3 oz (85g/⅓ cup) of margarine and seasonings.

2.   Chop the spinach finely in the pan with a pair of scissors when slightly cooled. Then add half the cream.

3.   Make a thick roux with 2 oz (55g/¼ cup) of margarine and the flour. Add the milk and the remainder of the cream. Beat thoroughly and season well.

4.   Separate the eggs. Allow the sauce to cool slightly and add the egg yolks. Stir well and add the spinach.

5.   Beat the egg whites stiffly and fold them into the spinach mixture.

6.   Pour into a greased loaf tin and bake in the oven at 375°F/190°C (Gas Mark 5) for 1 hour.

VEGETABLE RISOTTO

Imperial (Metric)	American
Olive oil	Olive oil
2 diced courgettes	2 diced zucchini
1 diced aubergine	1 diced eggplant
2 diced onions	2 diced onions
2 large cloves of garlic	2 large cloves of garlic
4 oz (115g) mushrooms	1 cup mushrooms
10 oz (285g) brown rice	1¼ cups brown rice
Sea salt and freshly ground black pepper	Sea salt and freshly ground black pepper
4 oz (115g) grated cheese	1 cup grated cheese
1 oz (30g) polyunsaturated margarine	2½ tablespoons polyunsaturated margarine

1.   Heat enough olive oil to sauté the diced courgettes (zucchini), aubergine (eggplant), and onions, and the garlic and sliced mushrooms. Stir constantly until soft.

2.   Add the rice and the seasonings and stir well.

3.   Remove the pan (skillet) from the heat and add 1½ pints (850ml/3¾ cups) of boiling water.

4.   Put in a flameproof casserole and cook gently for 45 minutes. Add the cheese and the margarine before serving.

VEGETARIAN STROGANOFF

Imperial (Metric)
1 large onion
4 sticks celery
¾ lb (340g) mushrooms
2 oz (55g) polyunsaturated
  margarine
1 tablespoon wholemeal flour
1 teaspoon yeast extract dissolved
  in ¼ pint (140ml) hot water
½ teaspoon thyme
Pinch of ground bayleaf
¼ pint (140ml) natural yogurt
Sea salt and freshly ground black
  pepper

American
1 large onion
4 stalks celery
¾ pound mushrooms
¼ cup polyunsaturated margarine
1 tablespoon wholewheat flour
1 teaspoon yeast extract dissolved
  in ⅔ cup hot water
½ teaspoon thyme
Pinch of ground bayleaf
⅔ cup plain yogurt
Sea salt and freshly ground black
  pepper

1. Slice the onion, celery, and mushrooms.

2. Sauté the onion and celery in the margarine for a few minutes. Add the mushrooms and cook for a further 2 minutes.

3. Stir in the flour. Add the yeast extract and water.

4. Bring to the boil. Add the herbs and simmer for 2-3 minutes.

5. Remove from the heat and add the yogurt. Heat slowly and serve with brown rice garnished with parsley.

STUFFED MUSHROOMS

Imperial (Metric)
12 large mushrooms
1 teaspoon sea salt
½ teaspoon freshly ground black
  pepper
1 oz (30g) polyunsaturated margarine
2 spring onions
1 tablespoon wholemeal flour
¼ pint (140ml) single cream
1½ tablespoons Parmesan cheese
½ cup chopped parsley

American
12 large mushrooms
1 teaspoon sea salt
½ teaspoon freshly ground black
  pepper
2½ tablespoons polyunsaturated
  margarine
2 scallions
1 tablespoon wholewheat flour
⅔ cup light cream
1½ tablespoons Parmesan cheese
½ cup chopped parsley

1. Wash mushrooms. Remove stalks and save them.

2. Grease an ovenproof dish and lay the mushrooms in hollow side up. Season with sea salt and black pepper.

3. Melt the margarine in a pan.

4. Chop the mushroom stalks and spring onions (scallions) and sauté in the margarine for about 3 minutes.

5. Reduce the heat and stir in the flour. Remove from the heat after 1 minute and carefully stir in the cream.

6. When smooth, return to the heat and cook until the mixture thickens. Stir in the chopped parsley and season.

7. Divide the mixture between the mushrooms, sprinkle with Parmesan, and cook for 15 minutes at 375°F/190°C (Gas Mark 5) until brown.

VEGETABLE CHARLOTTE

Imperial (Metric)	American
6 slices wholemeal bread	6 slices wholewheat bread
Polyunsaturated margarine	Polyunsaturated margarine
1 cup puréed carrots	1¼ cups puréed carrots
1 cup puréed turnips (or parsnips or swedes)	1¼ cups puréed turnips (or parsnips or rutabagas)
1 cup puréed Brussels sprouts	1¼ cups puréed Brussels sprouts

1. Spread the slices of wholemeal (wholewheat) bread with the margarine and cut into fingers.

2. Line a greased baking dish or pudding basin with the bread, reserving enough to cover the top.

3. Mix the puréed vegetables together and place in the dish. Cover with the remaining bread and bake for 30 minutes in a fairly hot oven, 400°F/200°C (Gas Mark 6).

VEGETABLE PIE

Imperial (Metric)	American
2 small carrots	2 small carrots
2 parsnips	2 parsnips
½ medium-sized swede	½ medium-sized rutabaga
1 small turnip	1 small turnip
1 onion	1 onion
2 medium-sized leeks	2 medium-sized leeks
4 oz (115g) runner beans	1 cup green beans
1½ lb (680g) potatoes	1½ pounds potatoes
½ pint (285ml) cheese sauce (page 117)	1½ cups cheese sauce (page 117)
2 oz (55g) polyunsaturated margarine	¼ cup polyunsaturated margarine
Sea salt and freshly ground black pepper	Sea salt and freshly ground black pepper

1. Peel and slice, or dice, all the vegetables finely.

2. Boil them in a small amount of salted water, adding the carrots a few minutes before the others as they take longer to cook.

3. Meanwhile, prepare and cook the potatoes separately. When they are almost tender, drain and slice them thinly.

4. When the other vegetables are cooked, drain them and place in a large, shallow, ovenproof dish. Pour the cheese sauce over them and mix thoroughly.

5. Lay the sliced potatoes in neat rows over the vegetable and sauce mixture. Dot with the margarine and sprinkle liberally with sea salt and black pepper.

6. Cook in a hot oven for 10-15 minutes and then, if the potatoes are not browned, place under a medium grill. Garnish with chopped parsley.

CABBAGE PIE

Imperial (Metric)
1 medium-sized white cabbage
3 oz (85g) polyunsaturated
    margarine
Pastry (short or flaky), enough to
    line and cover a 9-inch (23cm)
    pie dish
2 hard-boiled eggs
6 oz (170g) grated Cheddar cheese
Milk
Sea salt and freshly ground black
    pepper

American
1 medium-sized white cabbage
⅓ cup polyunsaturated margarine
Pastry (short or flaky), enough to
    line and cover a 9-inch pie dish
2 hard-boiled eggs
1½ cups grated Cheddar cheese
Milk
Sea salt and freshly ground black
    pepper

1. Shred the cabbage finely.

2. Melt the margarine in a large saucepan and add the shredded cabbage to it. Cook gently for about 5 minutes.

3. Line the pie dish with pastry and then build up alternate layers of cabbage, slices of hard-boiled egg, and grated cheese, seasoning each layer as you go. Repeat until the dish is full and cover with the remaining pastry.

4. Brush the top with milk and bake for about ½ an hour at 350°F/180°C (Gas Mark 4).

HOT BUTTON MUSHROOMS

Imperial (Metric)
1¼ lb (565g) button mushrooms
1 medium-sized onion
Olive oil
2 oz (55g) wholemeal flour
2 oz (55g) polyunsaturated
  margarine
½ pint (285ml) single cream
2 beaten eggs (free range)
White wine
Sea salt and freshly ground black
  pepper
1 8-inch (20cm) pastry case

American
1¼ pounds button mushrooms
1 medium-sized onion
Olive oil
½ cup wholewheat flour
¼ cup polyunsaturated margarine
1⅓ cups light cream
2 beaten eggs (free range)
White wine
Sea salt and freshly ground black
  pepper
1 8-inch pastry case

1. Clean and chop the mushrooms.

2. Dice the onion and sauté with the mushrooms in the oil. Put a few mushrooms aside for garnishing.

3. Add the flour and margarine to the remaining mixture and cook, stirring all the time.

4. Mix the cream, beaten eggs, white wine, and seasonings together. Add to the mushroom mixture.

5. Allow to cool then pour into the prepared pastry case and bake for about 30 minutes at 400°F/200°C (Gas Mark 6).

6. Garnish with the mushrooms you have saved and a few sprigs of parsley. Serve hot.

LENTIL PIE

Imperial (Metric)
6 oz (170g) lentils
1 tablespoon olive oil
1 tablespoon sunflower oil
1 onion

American
1 cup lentils
1 tablespoon olive oil
1 tablespoon sunflower oil
1 onion

1 tablespoon tomato purée	1 tablespoon tomato paste
1 tablespoon tomato ketchup	1 tablespoon tomato catsup
1 teaspoon vegetarian Worcester sauce	1 teaspoon vegetarian Worcester sauce
1 teaspoon yeast extract	1 teaspoon yeast extract
1 lb (455g) potatoes	1 pound potatoes
Top of the milk	Top of the milk
Sea salt and freshly ground black pepper	Sea salt and freshly ground black pepper
1 oz (30g) polyunsaturated margarine	2½ tablespoons polyunsaturated margarine
2 oz (55g) grated cheese	¼ cup grated cheese

1. Rinse and pick over the lentils. Place into a pan and just cover with water.

2. Add the olive oil and cook rapidly for 10 minutes, then simmer for about 15 minutes until a purée is formed.

3. Heat the sunflower oil. Chop the onion. Fry together until lightly brown.

4. Add the onion to the lentil mixture together with the tomato purée (paste), ketchup (catsup), yeast extract, Worcester sauce, sea salt, and black pepper.

5. Put the lentil mixture into an ovenproof dish and allow to cool. (This will solidify slightly and prevent the potato from sinking through the mixture when placed on top.)

6. Peel and cut the potatoes into even-sized pieces. Cook until soft.

7. Mash the potatoes with some top milk, margarine, and seasonings until light and fluffy. Spread carefully over the lentil mixture and sprinkle with grated cheese. Bake at 400°F/200°C (Gas Mark 6) for about 10 minutes until the cheese is golden brown.

SWEETCORN SOUFFLÉ

Imperial (Metric)
1 small tin of sweetcorn
2 oz (55g) polyunsaturated
  margarine
2 tablespoons wholemeal flour
½ pint (285ml) milk
Sea salt and freshly ground black
  pepper
Paprika
3 egg yolks
4 egg whites

American
1 small tin of sweetcorn
¼ cup polyunsaturated margarine
2 tablespoons wholewheat flour
1⅓ cups milk
Sea salt and freshly ground black
  pepper
Paprika
3 egg yolks
4 egg whites

1. Cook and drain the sweetcorn.

2. In a medium-sized saucepan, melt the margarine and add the
    flour to form a roux. Remove from the heat and gradually add
    the milk.

3. Season with sea salt, black pepper, and paprika. Return to the
    heat and cook gently, stirring constantly.

4. Allow to cool and add the sweetcorn. Mix in well and add 3 well-
    beaten egg yolks followed by 4 egg whites that have been whisked
    until stiff.

5. Fold in well and turn the mixture into a well-greased soufflé dish.
    Bake for 35-40 minutes at 350°F/180°C (Gas Mark 4) until well
    risen.

POTATO AND CHEESE LAYERS

Imperial (Metric)
2 lb (900g) potatoes
2 large onions
4 oz (115g) grated cheese
Polyunsaturated margarine
Sea salt and freshly ground black
  pepper
Top milk

American
2 pounds potatoes
2 large onions
1 cup grated cheese
Polyunsaturated margarine
Sea salt and freshly ground black
  pepper
Top milk

1. Peel the potatoes and boil them until they are almost cooked.

2. Meanwhile, prepare a large, flat ovenproof dish and peel and slice the onions thinly.

3. Drain the potatoes and slice them thinly.

4. Cover the base of the dish with the potatoes and sprinkle with grated cheese and some of the sliced onions. Dot with margarine, sea salt, and black pepper and cover with another layer of potatoes and onions.

5. Repeat until the dish is full, finishing with a layer of potatoes.

6. Pour a little top milk over the top so that it trickles down between the layers. Dot generously with margarine, sea salt, and black pepper and bake for ½ an hour at 375°F/190°C (Gas Mark 5), or until the potatoes begin to brown.

EASY OVEN OMELETTE

Imperial (Metric)	American
1 oz (30g) polyunsaturated margarine	2½ tablespoons polyunsaturated margarine
1 small onion	1 small onion
1 tomato	1 tomato
6 medium-sized mushrooms	6 medium-sized mushrooms
4 eggs (free range)	4 eggs (free range)
4 oz (115g) grated cheese	1 cup grated cheese
Sea salt and freshly ground black pepper	Sea salt and freshly ground black pepper

1. Heat the oven to 350°F/180°C (Gas Mark 4).

2. Place the margarine in a 7-inch (18cm) soufflé dish and place in the oven to melt. Chop the onion, tomato, and mushrooms, and add these to the dish. Leave to cook for a few minutes.

3. Whisk the eggs. Add the cheese and the seasonings, and pour carefully into the soufflé dish.

4. Cook for about 20 minutes until it is well risen and brown.

POTATO CAKES

Imperial (Metric)
½ lb (225g) wholemeal self-raising
  flour
1 teaspoon sea salt
3 oz (85g) polyunsaturated
  margarine
½ lb (225g) mashed potatoes
¼ cup milk
Caraway seeds

American
2 cups wholewheat self-raising flour
1 teaspoon sea salt
⅓ cup polyunsaturated margarine
1½ cups mashed potatoes
¼ cup milk
Caraway seeds

1. Mix the flour, salt, and margarine and add the mashed potatoes
    and enough milk to form a soft dough.

2. Roll on to a floured board to about ½ inch (1cm) thick and cut
    into ten or twelve rounds with a 3-inch (7.5cm) cutter.

3. Sprinkle with caraway seeds and bake on a greased baking sheet
    for 20-30 minutes at 400°F/200°C (Gas Mark 6).

Note: The dough can be prepared in advance. Eat the potato cakes
split and spread with butter or margarine. They make a satisfying
breakfast dish when served with mushrooms or grilled tomatoes.

HOT CHEESY POTATOES

Imperial (Metric)
6 large potatoes
½ pint (285ml) single cream
½ lb (225g) cottage cheese
1 teaspoon sea salt
3 spring onions (finely chopped)
2 cloves of garlic (finely chopped)
4 oz (115g) grated Cheddar cheese
Paprika

American
6 large potatoes
1⅓ cups light cream
1 cup cottage cheese
1 teaspoon sea salt
3 scallions (finely chopped)
2 cloves of garlic (finely chopped)
1 cup grated Cheddar cheese
Paprika

1. Boil the potatoes until they are just tender. Cut into small cubes.

2. Combine the cream, cottage cheese, salt, and spring onions (scallions) with the potatoes.

3. Put the mixture into a buttered ovenproof dish and sprinkle grated cheese and a little paprika over the top. Bake for about ½ an hour at 350°F/180°C (Gas Mark 4) and serve hot.

BROWN RICE, CHEESE AND LEEKS

Imperial (Metric)	American
2 cups water	2 cups water
2 oz (55g) polyunsaturated margarine	¼ cup polyunsaturated margarine
Sea salt	Sea salt
1 cup uncooked brown rice	1 cup uncooked brown rice
1 large onion	1 large onion
2 medium-sized leeks	2 medium-sized leeks
1 tablespoon single cream	1 tablespoon light cream
4 oz (115g) grated Cheddar cheese	1 cup grated Cheddar cheese
Freshly ground black pepper	Freshly ground black pepper
Chopped parsley to garnish	Chopped parsley to garnish

1. Bring 2 cups of water, 1 oz (30g/2½ tablespoons) margarine, and a little sea salt to the boil.

2. Add the brown rice, cover tightly, and simmer on a very low heat for 50 minutes.

3. Sauté the onion and the leeks in the remaining 1 oz (30g/2½ tablespoons) of margarine until they are cooked but not brown.

4. Place the cooked rice in a warm serving dish. Add the sautéed onion and leeks, the cream, the grated cheese, and seasoning to taste.

5. Place in a warm oven for 5-10 minutes so that the cheese is thoroughly melted. Garnish with parsley before serving.

Potatoes, Cheese and Eggs

Here are a few ideas for using up these common but nutritious items. They can be used for quick and easy lunches and also as the basis for more substantial evening meals, filled out with accompanying vegetables and perhaps home-made soup (see pages 93-101) to begin with.

POTATOES ROMANOV

Imperial (Metric)	American
6 large potatoes	6 large potatoes
1 small carton cottage cheese	1 small carton cottage cheese
1 clove of garlic	1 clove of garlic
3 spring onions	3 scallions
Sea salt	Sea salt
½ pint (285ml) sour cream	1⅓ cups sour cream
4 oz (115g) grated Cheddar cheese	1 cup grated Cheddar cheese
Paprika	Paprika

1. Peel the potatoes and boil them.

2. Cut the boiled potatoes into small neat cubes.

3. Mix the cottage cheese, the garlic clove (chopped finely), spring onions (scallions), sea salt to taste, and the sour cream. Combine with the potatoes.

4. Place the mixture in a well-greased casserole and sprinkle the top with the grated cheese.

5. Top with paprika and bake for about ½ an hour at 350°F/180°C (Gas Mark 4).

SPINACH AND EGG

Imperial (Metric)
½ lb (225g) chopped spinach
2 oz (55g) polyunsaturated margarine
½ lb (225g) cottage cheese
4 oz (115g) grated Parmesan cheese
¼ pint (140ml) double cream
3 beaten eggs (free range)
1 8-inch (20cm) blind cooked flan case

American
½ pound chopped spinach
¼ cup polyunsaturated margarine
1 cup cottage cheese
1 cup grated Parmesan cheese
⅔ cup heavy cream
3 beaten eggs (free range)
1 8-inch blind cooked flan case

1. Cook the spinach and drain well. Season and add the margarine.

2. Add the cottage cheese, Parmesan cheese, cream, and the beaten eggs. Mix thoroughly.

3. Spread the mixture in a blind cooked flan case and bake for about 40 minutes at 375°F/190°C (Gas Mark 5).

OEUFS FLORENTINE

Imperial (Metric)	American
½ lb (225g) fresh spinach	½ pound fresh spinach
2 eggs (free range)	2 eggs (free range)
¼ pint (140ml) cheese sauce (see page 117)	⅔ cup cheese sauce (see page 117)
¾ lb (340g) grated cheese	3 cups grated cheese
Sea salt and freshly ground black pepper	Sea salt and freshly ground black pepper

1. Cook the spinach and spread on the bottom of an ovenproof dish.

2. Make two wells in the centre of the spinach and crack an egg into each.

3. Spoon the cheese sauce over the spinach and eggs, sprinkle with the grated cheese and add seasonings as required.

4. Place in the oven and cook until the eggs are set (test them by gently moving aside the sauce with a knife) at 375°F/190°C (Gas Mark 5). Place under a hot grill to brown.

BAKED CHEESE EGGS

Imperial (Metric)	American
4 oz (115g) Cheddar cheese	4 ounces Cheddar cheese
1 oz (30g) polyunsaturated margarine	2½ tablespoons polyunsaturated margarine
4 eggs (free range)	4 eggs (free range)
Sea salt and freshly ground black pepper	Sea salt and freshly ground black pepper
4 tablespoons single cream	4 tablespoons light cream

1. Grate 2 oz (55g/½ cup) of the cheese and slice the remainder thinly.

2. Grease an ovenproof dish well with the margarine.

3. Cover the base of the dish with the cheese slices.

4. Break the eggs over the slices, taking care not to disturb the yolks.

5. Season with sea salt and black pepper and then pour the cream over the eggs. Sprinkle with the grated cheese and bake for 15 minutes at 425°F/220°C (Gas Mark 7). Brown under the grill.

CHEESE SOUFFLÉ

Imperial (Metric)
2 oz (55g) polyunsaturated
   margarine
2 oz (55g) wholemeal flour
¼ level teaspoon sea salt
¼ level teaspoon cayenne pepper
1 teaspoon mustard
½ pint (285ml) milk
3 large eggs (free range)
4 oz (115g) grated cheese

American
¼ cup polyunsaturated margarine
¼ cup wholewheat flour
¼ level teaspoon sea salt
¼ level teaspoon cayenne pepper
1 teaspoon mustard
1⅓ cups milk
3 large eggs (free range)
1 cup grated cheese

1. Make a roux by melting the margarine, then adding the flour and seasonings gradually.

2. Add the milk, stirring all the time, to form a smooth sauce.

3. Bring slowly to the boil and continue to cook for 1 minute. Set aside to cool.

4. Meanwhile, separate the eggs and beat the whites until they are stiff.

5. Whisk the yolks into the sauce and then fold in the grated cheese.

6. Using a metal spoon, gently fold the sauce into the egg whites and pour the mixture into a greased 7-inch (18cm) soufflé dish. Bake in the centre of the oven for 40-45 minutes at 375°F/190°C (Gas Mark 5). Serve immediately.

CHEESE PUDDING

Imperial (Metric)	American
2 oz (55g) fresh wholemeal breadcrumbs	1 cup fresh wholewheat breadcrumbs
4 oz (115g) grated cheese	1 cup grated cheese
1 teaspoon dried mustard	1 teaspoon dried mustard
Sea salt and freshly ground black pepper	Sea salt and freshly ground black pepper
2 eggs (free range)	2 eggs (free range)
¾ pint (425ml) milk	2 cups milk

1. Mix the breadcrumbs, cheese and seasonings lightly together.

2. Beat the eggs and milk together. Strain into the breadcrumb mixture.

3. Combine the ingredients well and pour into a greased ovenproof dish. Bake for ¾ hour at 350°F/180°C (Gas Mark 4).

All-Purpose Dishes

Finally, a mixed bag of recipes for quick and easy lunches or suppers, some of which may also be useful for entertaining visiting carnivores.

BASIC TOMATO FILLING
This can be used as the basis for a number of dishes.

Imperial (Metric)	American
1 large onion	1 large onion
1 tablespoon olive oil	1 tablespoon olive oil
1 small green pepper (or 3 medium leeks)	1 small green pepper (or 3 medium leeks)
1 tin tomatoes	1 can tomatoes
4 oz (115g) mushrooms	2 cups mushrooms
1 teaspoon sea salt	1 teaspoon sea salt
Freshly ground black pepper	Freshly ground black pepper
Pinch of mixed herbs	Pinch of mixed herbs
1 bay leaf	1 bay leaf
1 teaspoon tomato ketchup	1 teaspoon tomato catsup

1. Sauté the onion in the olive oil.

2. Add the green pepper (or leeks) and sauté for a further few minutes.

3. Add the tomatoes, chopping into lumps with kitchen scissors during cooking.

4. Add the seasonings and tomato ketchup (catsup). Simmer for 15 minutes. Remove the bay leaf.

MEATLESS LASAGNE

Imperial (Metric)	American
12 sheets wholemeal lasagne	12 sheets wholewheat lasagne
1 tablespoon vegetable oil	1 tablespoon vegetable oil
Grated cheese	Grated cheese
Basic tomato filling (see page 135)	Basic tomato filling (see page 135)
½ pint (285ml) cheese sauce (page 117)	1⅓ cups cheese sauce (page 117)

1. Cook the lasagne in boiling salted water to which the vegetable oil has been added (to prevent the strips of pasta sticking together) for 15 minutes. Drain.

2. Grease a suitable ovenproof dish and lay one layer of cooked pasta in the bottom. Cover with a layer of grated cheese and basic tomato filling, followed by another layer of pasta. Repeat until the dish is almost full. The last layer should be pasta.

3. Make the cheese sauce, with ½ pint (285ml/1⅓ cups) milk and pour over the lasagne. Sprinkle with grated cheese and bake for 15-20 minutes at 350°F/180°C (Gas Mark 4) until the top is brown.

RICE, NOODLES OR SPAGHETTI

1. Boil the required amount of pasta or rice in boiling salted water. Drain when *al dente*.

2. Replace in the saucepan, adding a tablespoon of margarine or vegetable oil.

3. Serve with the basic tomato filling (page 135) and grated cheese.

MEATLESS POTATO MOUSSAKA

Imperial (Metric)	**American**
4/5 medium-sized potatoes	4/5 medium-sized potatoes
Basic tomato filling (see page 135)	Basic tomato filling (see page 135)
½ pint (285ml) cheese sauce (page 117)	1⅓ cups cheese sauce (page 117)
1 egg (free range)	1 egg (free range)
1 teaspoon grated nutmeg	1 teaspoon grated nutmeg
Grated cheese	Grated cheese

1. Cook the potatoes until they are almost done. Slice lengthways.

2. Cover the bottom of a suitable greased ovenproof dish with the potatoes and pour in enough tomato filling to cover them. Lay another layer of potatoes over, followed by more filling, finishing with a layer of potatoes.

3. Make a basic cheese sauce using ½ pint (285ml/1⅓ cups) milk. Remove from the heat when cooked and add one whisked egg and the grated nutmeg.

4. Pour the sauce over the potatoes. Sprinkle with grated cheese and cook for ½ hour at 375°F/190°C (Gas Mark 5).

CHINESE NOODLES

Imperial (Metric)	American
½ lb (225g) medium egg noodles (Chow Mein noodles)	2 cups medium egg noodles (Chow Mein noodles)
Vegetable oil	Vegetable oil
½ lb (225g) beansprouts (lightly boiled or fried)	4 cups beansprouts (lightly boiled or fried)
4 chopped spring onions	4 chopped scallions
1 cup cooked peas	1 cup cooked peas
1 tablespoon soya sauce	1 tablespoon soy sauce
1 tablespoon very dry sherry	1 tablespoon very dry sherry
1 teaspoon ground ginger	1 teaspoon ground ginger
4 oz (115g) toasted cashew nuts	1 cup toasted cashew nuts

1. Boil the noodles until they are tender.

2. Heat some vegetable oil in a large frying pan or wok. Add the beansprouts, chopped spring onions (scallions), and cooked peas.

3. Stir fry until just tender. Add soya (soy) sauce and dry sherry. Sprinkle with ginger and mix well.

4. Add the noodles and cashew nuts. Mix gently. Garnish with parsley and serve with crisply-cooked cabbage.

STUFFED PANCAKES

Batter:

Imperial (Metric)	American
4 oz (115g) wholemeal flour	1 cup wholewheat flour
Pinch of sea salt	Pinch of sea salt
1 egg (free range)	1 egg (free range)
½ pint (285ml) milk	1⅓ cups milk

Filling:

Imperial (Metric)	**American**
2 oz (55g) sliced button mushrooms	¾ cup sliced button mushrooms
1 small onion	1 small onion
2 oz (55g) polyunsaturated margarine	¼ cup polyunsaturated margarine
1 oz (30g) wholemeal flour	¼ cup wholewheat flour
½ pint (285ml) milk	1⅓ cups milk
6 oz (170g) grated hard cheese	1½ cups grated hard cheese
Sea salt and freshly ground black pepper	Sea salt and freshly ground black pepper

1. For the batter, sieve the flour and salt into a basin. Beat the egg and milk gradually into the centre until the batter is smooth. Allow to stand.

2. Fry the mushrooms and onion gently in the margarine.

3. Remove the mushrooms and onion and add the 1 oz (30g/¼ cup) of flour to the melted margarine that remains.

4. Gradually add the milk, stirring all the time, and cook for 1 minute. Remove from the heat and put back the mushrooms and onion, together with the grated cheese and seasonings.

5. Use the batter to make 8 thin pancakes in an 8-inch (20cm) heavy-based frying pan and keep them warm by placing them on a plate standing on a pan of hot water. Place a piece of greased greaseproof paper between each pancake.

6. Place a tablespoon of the filling onto each pancake. Fold into four, arrange on a warm dish, and serve immediately.

LASAGNE ROLLS

Imperial (Metric)
8 lasagne sheets
1 tablespoon vegetable oil
Sea salt

American
8 lasagne sheets
1 tablespoon vegetable oil
Sea salt

Filling:

Imperial (Metric)
½ lb (225g) chopped spinach
2 tablespoons grated Parmesan
  cheese
½ lb (225g) cottage cheese
Pinch of grated nutmeg
Sea salt and freshly ground black
  pepper

American
½ pound chopped spinach
2 tablespoons grated Parmesan
  cheese
1 cup cottage cheese
Pinch of grated nutmeg
Sea salt and freshly ground black
  pepper

Sauce:

Imperial (Metric)
2 large onions
1 clove of garlic
2 tablespoons vegetable oil
1 tin of tomatoes
2 tablespoons tomato ketchup
1 teaspoon mixed herbs
4 oz (115g) grated cheese

American
2 large onions
1 clove of garlic
2 tablespoons vegetable oil
1 can of tomatoes
2 tablespoons tomato catsup
1 teaspoon mixed herbs
1 cup grated cheese

1. Cook the lasagne in boiling water, to which the vegetable oil and some sea salt have been added, for 10 minutes. Drain and separate the sheets and lay them on some kitchen paper.

2. Cook the spinach. Drain well. Add the cheeses, nutmeg, sea salt and black pepper, mixing well.

3. Divide the mixture equally between the lasagne sheets. Spread and roll up. Arrange the rolls on end, packed closely together in a greased ovenproof dish.

4. Make the sauce by peeling the onions and the garlic and chopping them finely. Then sauté them in the vegetable oil for about 5 minutes. Add the tomatoes, mixed herbs, and the ketchup (catsup). Boil and then simmer for about 5 minutes.

5. Pour the sauce over the lasagne rolls. Sprinkle with grated cheese and cook for about an hour at 350°F/180°C (Gas Mark 4).

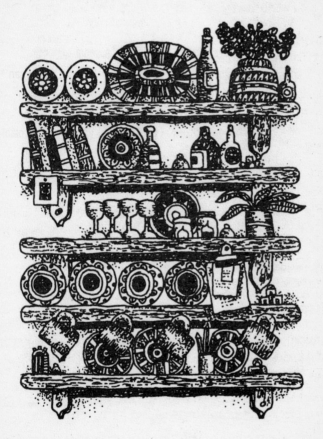

NUT ROAST

Imperial (Metric)	American
1 large chopped onion	1 large chopped onion
1 tablespoon polyunsaturated margarine	1 tablespoon polyunsaturated margarine
1 cup ground mixed nuts	1¼ cup ground mixed nuts
1 cup fresh wholemeal breadcrumbs	1¼ cup fresh wholewheat breadcrumbs
1 cup cooked brown rice	1¼ cup cooked brown rice
1 teaspoon yeast extract	1 teaspoon yeast extract
1 teaspoon ready-made horseradish sauce	1 teaspoon ready-made horseradish sauce
Sea salt and freshly ground black pepper to taste	Sea salt and freshly ground black pepper to taste
1 teaspoon mustard	1 teaspoon mustard
Fresh herbs, as desired	Fresh herbs, as desired

1. Sauté the chopped onion in the margarine but do not allow it to brown.

2. Mix the nuts, breadcrumbs, brown rice, the yeast extract dissolved in a cup of boiling water, horseradish sauce, and seasonings in a large bowl. Add the sautéed onion.

3. Mix well with the hands and place on a greased baking dish. Shape to resemble a loaf.

4. Sprinkle with more breadcrumbs and dot with margarine. Bake for about 40 minutes at 400°F/200°C (Gas Mark 6). Serve as a traditional British Sunday lunch, with roast potatoes, non-meat gravy, and vegetables.

Use this recipe as a filling for the following.

STUFFED CABBAGE LEAVES

Imperial (Metric)
Nut mixture (page 142)
8 large cabbage leaves
Homemade tomato sauce/non-meat
  gravy

American
Nut mixture (page 142)
8 large cabbage leaves
Homemade tomato sauce/non-meat
  gravy

1. Make the nut mixture as described on page 142.

2. Blanch 8 large cabbage leaves for about 12 minutes in boiling salted water. Drain and pat dry with kitchen paper.

3. Place a tablespoon of the nut mixture on each leaf. Tuck in the sides and roll up to form a parcel.

4. Place the leaves in a large ovenproof dish and soak either with homemade tomato sauce or with non-meat gravy. Cover the dish and bake for 40 minutes at 350°F/180°C (Gas Mark 4). A tablespoon of red wine can be added to the sauce or to the gravy.

PASTITSIO

Imperial (Metric)	American
1 medium-sized onion	1 medium-sized onion
1 clove of garlic	1 clove of garlic
3 tablespoons vegetable oil	3 tablespoons vegetable oil
1 oz (30g) polyunsaturated margarine	2½ tablespoons polyunsaturated margarine
3 oz (85g) lentils	½ cup lentils
1 tin of tomatoes	1 can of tomatoes
1 tablespoon tomato ketchup	1 tablespoon tomato catsup
Large pinch of cinnamon	Large pinch of cinnamon
½ teaspoon mixed herbs	½ teaspoon mixed herbs
Sea salt and freshly ground black pepper	Sea salt and freshly ground black pepper
8 oz (225g) mixed pasta shapes	4 cups mixed pasta shapes
6 oz (170g) mushrooms	3 cups mushrooms
Grated cheese	Grated cheese

Sauce:

Imperial (Metric)	American
1 oz (30g) polyunsaturated margarine	2½ tablespoons polyunsaturated margarine
1 oz (30g) wholemeal flour	¼ cup wholewheat flour
½ pint (285ml) milk	1⅓ cups milk
2 beaten eggs (free range)	2 beaten eggs (free range)

1. Peel and chop the onion finely. Peel the garlic and crush to a smooth paste with a little sea salt.

2. Heat the vegetable oil and margarine in a large saucepan, sauté the onions and garlic, and add the lentils with enough water to cover them. Cover and cook gently for about 30 minutes.

3. When the lentils are soft add the (chopped) tomatoes, ketchup (catsup), cinnamon, herbs, sea salt and black pepper. Cook uncovered until reduced by half.

4. Meanwhile, cook the pasta shapes in boiling salted water until they are just tender. Drain well. Wash and slice the mushrooms.

5. For the sauce, melt the margarine in a small pan. Stir in the flour, gradually add the milk (stirring all the time), and simmer for 2-3 minutes. Remove from heat and allow to cool slightly. Add the beaten eggs and season to taste.

6. Grease a large ovenproof dish and put in alternate layers of pasta, lentil and tomato mixture, and sliced raw mushrooms, finishing with a layer of lentils and tomato. Pour the sauce over the last layer and sprinkle with grated cheese. Cook for ½ hour at 400°F/200°C (Gas Mark 6) or until golden brown.

STUFFED RED PEPPERS

Imperial (Metric)	American
4 medium-sized red peppers	4 medium-sized red peppers
1 cup fresh wholemeal breadcrumbs	1¼ cup fresh wholemeal breadcrumbs
4 oz (115g) grated cheese	1 cup grated cheese
4 oz (115g) ground walnuts	1 cup ground walnuts
2 tablespoons tarragon	2 tablespoons tarragon
Seasoning	Seasoning
1 egg (free range)	1 egg (free range)
Milk	Milk

1. Remove the tops of the peppers and take out the seeds.

2. Combine the breadcrumbs, grated cheese and the walnuts. Add the tarragon and seasoning.

3. Beat the egg into the mixture and gradually add enough milk to make the mixture sticky but not too wet.

4. Stuff the peppers with the mixture. Either replace the tops or fill the hole with breadcrumbs mixed with grated cheese topped with a whole walnut.

5. Place the stuffed peppers in an ovenproof dish. They should stand in about ½ inch (1cm) of water. Cover the dish and cook in the oven for about 15 minutes. Uncover and cook for another 30 minutes, or until the peppers are tender, at 350°F/180°C (Gas Mark 4).

CHESTNUT AND SPROUT PIE

Pastry:

Imperial (Metric)
6 oz (170g) wholemeal flour
2 oz (55g) grated cheese
2 oz (55g) sunflower seeds
Seasoning
½ lb (225g) polyunsaturated
  margarine

American
1¼ cups wholewheat flour
½ cup grated cheese
½ cup sunflower seeds
Seasoning
1 cup polyunsaturated margarine

Filling:

Imperial (Metric)
1 lb (455g) Brussels sprouts
½ lb (225g) chestnuts
2 oz (55g) polyunsaturated
  margarine
1 teaspoon mixed herbs
2 cloves of garlic
½ lb (225g) onions
2 oz (55g) wholemeal flour
2 oz (55g) grated cheese
Seasoning

American
1 pound Brussels sprouts
½ pound chestnuts
¼ cup polyunsaturated margarine
1 teaspoon mixed herbs
2 cloves of garlic
½ pound onions
½ cup wholewheat flour
½ cup grated cheese
Seasoning

1. *Pastry:* Mix the flour, cheese, and sunflower seeds together. Add seasoning. Rub in the margarine and some water until the pastry binds. Keep in the refrigerator.

2. *Filling:* Clean the sprouts and blanch in boiling water. Save the stock.

3. Shell the chestnuts by cutting cross-like incisions on them and boiling them for about 5 minutes: the shells will then come off easily.

4. Place the chestnuts in a deep pie dish with the sprouts. Melt the margarine in a pan and then add the mixed herbs, garlic, and onions. Cook gently for 5 minutes. Add the flour and mix in well.

5. Take the pan off the heat and add the sprout stock. Stir well, return to the heat and continue to stir until the mixture thickens.

6. Add the grated cheese and stir in. Pour over the sprouts and chestnuts. Season to taste.

7. Roll out the pastry to about ¼-inch (5mm) thickness. Place over the top of the pie and bake in the oven for about 40 minutes at 400°F/200°C (Gas Mark 6).

REFERENCES

Chapter 1: Breaking the Mould

1. Douglas Hill, *Man, Myth and Magic,* p. 2929.
2. Plutarch, *Moralia,* tr. H. Cherniss and W. C. Helmbold (1957).
3. The quotations in this section are from Hesketh Pearson, *G.B.S. A Full Length Portrait* (1942).
4. C. L. Dodgson, *Some Popular Fallacies About Vivisection,* in *Lewis Carroll: The Complete Works* (1977).

Chapter 2: The Ethical Diet

1. Brigid Brophy, 'The Rights of Animals' (*Sunday Times/Vegetarian Society, 1965*).
2. Akers, *Vegetarian Sourcebook,* p. 153.
3. Bentham, *Principles of Morals and Legislation.*
4. Singer, *Animal Liberation,* p. 3.
5. Kathleen Lennon, rev. of Frey's *Rights, Killing and Suffering* in the *TLS,* 1984.
6. *The Vegan,* XXVII, Spring 1980.
7. Quoted by Victoria Moran, *Compassion,* p. 28.
8. Moran, op. cit., p. 29.
9. Singer, *Animal Liberation,* pp. 96, 191-2.
10. Dombrowski, *The Philosophy of Vegetarianism,* p. 4.

Chapter 3: Staying Alive

1. Article in *Mademoiselle* magazine; quoted by Rodger Doyle, *Vegetarian Handbook,* p. 19.
2. Doyle, ibid., p. 71.
3. Ibid.
4. L. Jean Bogert et al, *Nutrition and Physical Fitness* (1973), p. 96.

5. Sussman, *Vegetarian Alternative*, p. 86.
6. See Gary Null, *Protein for Vegetarians* (1975), p. 52.
7. Akers, *Vegetarian Sourcebook*, p. 24.
8. Ibid, p. 30.
9. Ibid, p. 33.
10. Monica L. Rice, *Vegetarian Times*, September/October 1977.
11. R. D. Bargen, *The Vegetarian's Self-Defence Manual* (1979), p. 97.
12. Bronwen Humphreys, *The Vegetarian*, September/October 1983.
13. John A. Scharffenberg, *Problems With Meat*, p. 82.
14. Michael J. Hill, 'Bacteria and the Aetiology of Cancer of the Large Bowel', *The Lancet* (1971).
15. R. L. Phillips et al, 'Coronary Heart Disease Mortality among Seventh-day Adventists . . .', *American Journal of Clinical Nutrition* (1978).
16. Scharffenberg, op. cit., p. 24.
17. Akers, op. cit., p. 72.
18. R. L. Phillips, 'Role of Lifestyle and Dietary Habits in Risk of Cancer among Seventh-day Adventists', *Cancer Research* (November 1975).

Chapter 4: Counting the Cost

1. Jon Wynne-Tyson, *Food for a Future*, p. 17.
2. Peter Burwash and John Tullio, *Peter Burwash's Vegetarian Primer*, p. 70.
3. Akers, *Vegetarian Handbook*.
4. Dan Taylor, quoted in *Vegetarian Times*, May/June 1979, p. 32.
5. Peter Roberts, Foreword to Anna Roberts, *The Magic Bean*, p. 15.
6. *Plain Truth* (Pasadena, California), March 1973; quoted by Singer, *Animal Liberation*, p. 116.
7. Compassion in World Farming leaflet, 'Factory Farm '79. What You Can Do'.
8. Peter Burwash, op. cit., p. 64.
9. *The New Vegetarian*, February 1978, p. 27.
10. Interview with Linda McCartney by Jack Thompson, *The Vegetarian*, July/August 1984.
11. Editorial, *The Vegetarian*, May/June 1984, p. 16.
12. *Meat Trades Journal*, 12 April 1984.
13. *Here's Health*, March 1985.

READING LIST

GENERAL WORKS

Keith Akers, *A Vegetarian Sourcebook* (1983).

Nathaniel Altman, *Eating For Life* (1973).

Animal Welfare in Poultry, Pig and Veal Calf Production (HMSO, 1981).

Janet Barkas, *The Vegetable Passion* (1975).

Louis Berman, *Vegetarianism and the Jewish Tradition* (1982).

Brigid Brophy, 'The Rights of Animals' (*Sunday Times*/Vegetarian Society, 1965).

Peter Burwash and John Tullius, *Peter Burwash's Vegetarian Primer* (1983).

Stephen R. L. Clark, *The Moral Status of Animals* (1977).

——, *The Nature of the Beast: Are Animals Moral?* (1982).

Marian Stamp Dawkins, *Animal Suffering* (1980).

Daniel Dombrowski, *Vegetarianism: The Philosophy Behind The Ethical Diet* (1985).

Rodger Doyle, *The Vegetarian Handbook* (1980).

Michael W. Fox, *Returning to Eden: Animal Rights and Human Responsibility* (1980).

Dudley Giehl, *Vegetarianism: A Way of Life* (1981).

Stanley and Roslind Godlovitch and John Harris (eds.), *Animals, Men and Morals: An Enquiry into the Mal-treatment of Non-Humans* (1972).

Donal Griffin, *The Question of Animal Awareness* (1976).

Maurice Hanssen, *E for Additives* (1984).

Ruth Harrison, *Animal Machines* (1964).

Clive Hollands, *Compassion is the Bugler* (1981).

Andrew Linzey, *Animal Rights: A Christian Assessment of Man's Treatment of Animals* (1976).

Charles Magel, *A Bibliography on Animal Rights and Related Matters* (1981).

Jim Mason and Peter Singer, *Animal Factories* (1980).

Mary Midgley, *Animals and Why They Matter: A Journey Round the Species Barrier* (1984).

Victoria Moran, *Compassion: The Ultimate Ethic* (1985).

R. K. Morris and M. W. Fox (eds.), *On the Fifth Day: Animal Rights and Human Ethics* (1978).

Richard North, *The Animals Report* (1984).

David Paterson and Richard D. Ryder (eds.), *Animal Rights: A Symposium* (1979).

Tom Regan, *All That Dwells Therein* (1982).

——, *The Case for Animal Rights* (1983).

Tom Regan and Peter Singer (eds.), *Animal Rights and Human Obligations* (1976).

Report of the Technical Committee to Enquire into the Welfare of Animals Kept Under Intensive Livestock Husbandry Systems [the Brambell Report] (HMSO, 1965).

Richard Ryder, *Victims of Science* (1975).

Henry S. Salt, *Animals' Rights* (1882).

John A. Scharffenberg, *Problems With Meat* (1979).

Peter Singer, *Animal Liberation: Towards an End to Man's Inhumanity to Animals* 1976, 1983).

Vic Sussman, *The Vegetarian Alternative* (1978).

E. S. Turner, *All Heaven in a Rage* (1964).

Esmé Wynne-Tyson, *The Philosophy of Compassion* (1970).

Jon Wynne-Tyson, *The Civilized Alternative* (1972).

——, *Food for a Future* (1975, 1979).

COOKBOOKS

Unless otherwise stated, the following are all published by Thorsons, the largest publishers of vegetarian cookbooks in the world and official publishers for the Vegetarian Society (UK).

1. *General*

Jenny Allday, *Desserts, Cheese-cakes and Gateaux* (1984).

——, *Ice Cream, Sorbets, Mousses and Parfaits* (1982).

Pamela Brown, *Vegetarian Cookertop Cookery* (1985).

Sarah Brown, *The Vegetarian Kitchen* (BBC, 1984).

Margaret Cousins and Jill Metcalfe, *The Vegetarian on a Diet* (1984).

Desda Crockett, *Salads* (1983).

Pamela Dixon, *The Bean and Lentil Cookbook* (1982).

——, *Pies, Bakes and Casseroles* (1983).

Rose Elliot, *Bean Feast* (White Eagle, 1975).

——, *Book of Vegetables* (Fontana, 1983).

——, *Foreign Flavour: Vegetarian Dishes of the World* (Fontana, 1982).

——, *Gourmet Vegetarian Cooking* (Collins, 1982).
——, *Not Just a Load of Old Lentils* (Fontana, 1976).
——, The Vegetarian Baby Book (Vegetarian Society, 1981).
David Eno, *The Vegetarian Barbecue* (1984).
Evelyn Findlater, *Evelyn Findlater's Vegetarian Food Processor* (1985).
Nikki and David Goldbeck, *The Complete Wholefood Cuisine* (1984).
Rachael Holme, *Better Breakfasts* (1982).
Janet Hunt, *Pizzas and Pancakes* (1982).
——, *Quiches and Flans* (1982).
——, *Pasta Dishes* (1982).
——, *A Vegetarian in the Family* (1984).
——, *Vegetarian Snacks and Starters* (1984).
Janet Hunt (ed.), *The Very Best of Vegetarian Cooking* (1984).
Leah Leneman, *The Amazing Avocado* (1984).
Leon Lewis, *Vegetarian Dinner Parties* (1983).
Jo Marcangelo, *Creative Cheese Cookery* (1985).
Jane O'Brien, *The Magic of Tofu* (1983).
Anna Roberts, *The Magic Bean* [using soya protein] (1985).
Craig and Ann Sams, *The Brown Rice Cookbook* (1983).
Martha Rose Shulman, *Fast Vegetarian Feasts* (1983).
——, *Garlic Cookery* (1984).
——, *Herb and Honey Cookery* (1984).
——, *The Vegetarian Feast* (1982).
Kathy Silk, *First Steps in Vegetarian Cooking* (1983).
Colin Spencer, *Colin Spencer's Cordon Vert* (1985).
Susan Thorpe, *The Four Seasons Wholefood Cookbook* (1983).
Lorraine Whiteside, *The Carob Cookbook* (1984).

2. *Regional and Vegan*
Eva Batt, *Eva Batt's Vegan Cookery* (1985).
Alkmini Chaitow, *Greek Vegetarian Cooking* (1982).
Jean Conil, with Fay Franklin, *Jean Conil's Cuisine Végétarienne Française* (1985).
Rose Friedman, *Jewish Vegetarian Cooking* (1984).
Leah Leneman, *Vegan Cooking* (1982).
Jo Marcangelo, *Italian Vegetarian Cooking* (1984).
Edith Metcalfe de Plata, *Mexican Vegetarian Cooking* (1983).
Michael Pandya, *Michael Pandya's Indian Vegetarian Cooking* (1985).

USEFUL ADDRESSES

United Kingdom

The Vegetarian Society (UK)
(1) Parkdale
     Dunham Road
     Altrincham
     Cheshire WA14 4QG

(2) 53 Marloes Road
     London W8 6LA

The Vegan Society
47 Highlands Road
Leatherhead
Surrey

National Anti-Vivisection Society
51 Harley Street
London W1N 1DD

Compassion in World Farming
Lyndum House
High Street
Petersfield
Hampshire

Animal Aid
111 High Street
Tonbridge
Kent

Beauty Without Cruelty
1 Calverley Park
Tunbridge Wells
Kent TN1 2SG

The International Jewish Vegetarian Society
853/855 Finchley Road
London NW11 8LX

United States

Friends of Animals Inc.
11 West 60th Street
New York NY 10023

American Vegan Society
501 Old Harding Highway
Malaga
NJ 08328

Beauty Without Cruelty
175 West 12th Street
New York NY 10012

Animal Rights Network
P.O. Box 5234
Westport
Ct. 06880

Australia

Animal Liberation
Total Environment Centre
18 Argyle Street
Sydney
NSW 2000

New Zealand

Save Animals From Experimentation
P.O. Box 647
Auckland 1

GENERAL INDEX

RECIPE INDEX